Mastering the Science of Organizational Chan

Inspiring the Next Game: Strategy Ideas for Forward Looking Leaders

BCG Henderson Institute

Mastering the Science of Organizational Change

Edited by
Martin Reeves and Kevin Whitaker

DE GRUYTER

ISBN 978-3-11-069771-1
e-ISBN (PDF) 978-3-11-069783-4
e-ISBN (EPUB) 978-3-11-069794-0
ISSN 2701-8857

Library of Congress Control Number: 2020949347

Bibliographic information published by the Deutsche Nationalbibliothek
The Deutsche Nationalbibliothek lists this publication in the Deutsche Nationalbibliografie;
detailed bibliographic data are available on the Internet at http://dnb.dnb.de.

© 2021 Walter de Gruyter GmbH, Berlin/Boston
Cover image: sesame/DigitalVision Vectors/Getty Images
Typesetting: Integra Software Services Pvt. Ltd.
Printing and binding: CPI books GmbH, Leck

www.degruyter.com

Acknowledgments

We would like to acknowledge all of the authors whose work appears on the following pages: Vikram Bhalla, Hans-Paul Bürkner, Rodolphe Charme di Carlo, Tom Deegan, Diana Dosik, Lars Fæste, Jack Fuller, Kaelin Goulet, Ashley Grice, Knut Haanæs, Gerry Hansell, Fabien Hassan, Jim Hemerling, Stephanie Hurder, Perry Keenan, Jens Kengelbach, Julie Kilmann, Ryoji Kimura, Julien Legrand, Ib Löfgrén, Hen Lotan, Yulia Lyusina, Dave Matthews, Stéphanie Mingardon, Harshal Parikh, Martin Reeves, Shaheer Rizvi, Mike Shanahan, Peter Tollman, Gideon Walter, and Kevin Whitaker. We would also like to acknowledge our academic collaborator Simon Levin, the James S. McDonnell Distinguished University Professor in Ecology and Evolutionary Biology at Princeton University, who co-authored several of these articles and has helped deepen our thinking on the larger Science of Change topic.

We would also like to acknowledge the broader BCG Henderson Institute community: our Fellows, Ambassadors, and operations teams over the years, who have all made invaluable contributions to our research; our academic collaborators, who have expanded our horizons of new ideas; and our BCG practice area partners, especially the TURN and Transformation practice, and the Corporate Finance & Strategy practice, who have partnered on several of these articles.

https://doi.org/10.1515/9783110697834-202

About the BCG Henderson Institute

The BCG Henderson Institute is the Boston Consulting Group's think tank, dedicated to exploring and developing valuable new insights from business, technology, economics, and science by embracing the powerful technology of ideas. The Institute engages leaders in provocative discussion and experimentation to expand the boundaries of business theory and practice and to translate innovative ideas from within and beyond business.

https://doi.org/10.1515/9783110697834-203

Contents

Introduction

A rapidly evolving business context, driven by accelerating technological, political, and social change, is motivating an increasing strategic priority for business leaders to enact large-scale organizational change. At any one time, about one-third of large US companies are experiencing a significant multi-year decline in their ability to create shareholder value. Within *that* group, one-third fail to recover within the following five years. Even companies that are current industry leaders are vulnerable to disruption. Even the new leader of a top-performing company needs to watch over their shoulder for – and transform the company in anticipation of – the next disruption. In other words, if the company ain't broke, fix it preemptively anyway.

Even if companies recognize the need to preempt disruption by others with self-disruption, the odds of success in large-scale change are not good. This book is about how to beat the odds in large-scale change management using an evidence-based approach. It is an extensive analysis of what approaches actually work in which circumstances, based on our evaluation of hundreds of companies. It summarizes the work of the BCG Henderson Institute and its Fellows and Ambassadors across several years to develop a more scientific approach to change.

The book is divided into three sections. First, we discuss the imperatives for self-disruption. Second, we discuss how to manage the process of change. Finally, we close by discussing how organizations can take change to the next level.

In section one, Chapter 1 shows why it is better to transform preemptively rather than during or after a crisis and lays out six imperatives for preemptive transformation. In Chapters 2 to 7 we explore each of these imperatives in detail, examining the need to (1) adopt a "biological" mindset that embraces the complexity and uncertainty of change, (2) create a sense of urgency in the organization, (3) adopt metrics that assess your readiness for the future, (4) develop sustained transformation capabilities, (5) become a purpose-driven company, and (6) understand which pathway to transformation is most suitable to your situation.

In the second section, we discuss ways to manage the process of change. Chapter 8 lays out the main reasons why change management fails and shares a smart and simple approach to target these failure points. Chapter 9 goes on to examine quantitatively which specific factors increase the chance of transformation success. In Chapter 10, we translate these lessons into a concrete action plan for CEOs. Chapter 11 explores how to decide when you should transform, and in Chapter 12 we shift our focus to examine how to effectively turn around an M&A target in distress.

https://doi.org/10.1515/9783110697834-205

In the final section, we address some specific new challenges and opportunities for leaders to take change to the next level, Chapter 13 shows how companies can adopt an "always-on" mentality to transformation. Chapter 14 dives into the role of creativity and counterfactual thinking, and the value of playing games, to think about strategy and transformation in a different way. Chapter 15 studies how a holistic, human-centric approach can make change programs more successful. Chapter 16 digs into digital transformations, and Chapter 17 concludes with a view on how to make sure that your transformation leads to sustained, long-term growth.

We hope that this book helps guide leaders in making the right choices when it comes to one of the highest-stakes bets they will likely make – large-scale change.

Part I: **Six Steps to Successful Preemptive Change**

Martin Reeves, Lars Fæste, Fabien Hassan, Harshal Parikh, and Kevin Whitaker

Chapter 1
Preemptive Transformation: Fix it Before it Breaks

Cure the disease that has not yet happened. — *Chinese saying*

In business transformations, there are plausible reasons to believe that time is an essential factor. Companies that change early may get a first-mover advantage, acting ahead of their competitors and potential disruptors. Besides, business organizations are complex systems, which often decline much faster than they grow,[1] an asymmetry that has been called the *Seneca effect*. This is driven by the fact that complicated systems are composed of many variables with nonlinear feedback loops, which can lead to sudden and unpredictable transitions and collapse. Considering that transformations take time, moving preemptively may be the best way to prevent obsolescence and collapse.

Leaders may be reluctant to change their companies when they are in a comfortable position and they may understandably feel little urgency to change when current performance indicators are still healthy. Transformations are costly, monopolize management attention, and may create distraction or instability, leading many to follow the adage: "If it ain't broke, don't fix it."

So, should business leaders engage in transformation preemptively or wait for a degradation of performance to trigger change? To answer this, we leveraged an evidence-based approach to transformation (Chapter 9).[2]

We analyzed hundreds of transformations involving restructuring costs launched between 2010 and 2014 by large listed US companies[3] and we found

---

1 Martin Reeves, Simon Levin, and Kevin Whitaker, "Leaping Before the Platform Burns: The Increasing Necessity of Preemptive Innovation," *BCG Henderson Institute*, April 25, 2018. https://www.bcg.com/publications/2018/leaping-before-platform-burns-increasing-necessity-preemptive-innovation [accessed 9/5/2020].

2 Hans-Paul Bürkner, Lars Fæste, Jim Hemerling, Yulia Lyusina, and Martin Reeves, "The Transformations That Work – and Why," BCG Publications, November 7, 2017. https://www.bcg.com/publications/2017/transformations-people-organization-that-work-why [accessed 9/5/2020].

3 Analysis includes all US companies that reached a market capitalization of $5 billion at least once during the considered time frame, excluding companies in energy (owing to the volatility of energy prices) and real estate (owing to an insufficient number of firms for benchmarking

https://doi.org/10.1515/9783110697834-001

that preemptive change does indeed generate significantly higher long-term value than reactive change, and it does so faster and more reliably.

The Value of Preemptive Transformation

Because each company's circumstances are unique, we studied relative financial performance to identify preemption, rather than making qualitative timing judgments. If a company embarks on a transformation when it is outperforming its industry – as measured by TSR (total shareholder return) over the past year – the transformation can be described as preemptive. On the other hand, a transformation is categorized as reactive if it is launched while the firm is underperforming its industry on the basis of TSR.

Our analysis shows that in the three years following the start of a transformation, preemptive transformers have an annualized TSR that is 3 percentage points higher than that of reactive transformers. Outperformance following a preemptive transformation is true not only in the aggregate but across most industries, except in financial services (see Figure 1.1). In the period of our analysis, the financial

In most industries, Pre-emptive transformation creates more value

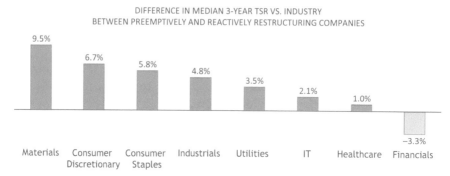

Note: Based on GICS industry classification. Excludes industries with less than 40 observed transformations
Source: Compustat, S&P Capital IQ, BCG Henderson Institute

Figure 1.1: The Difference in Median 3-Year TSR by Industry Between Companies that Restructure Preemptively and Those That Restructure Reactively.

performance); transformations are indicated by the appearance of restructuring costs in the company's quarterly accounts (N = 608).

sector was still recovering from the crisis and the subsequent regulatory changes, which may have caused anomalies.

Is this outperformance explained simply by the tendency of high-performing firms to continue outperforming? In fact, for companies that do not transform, there is no observable link between past and future long-term TSR. A small "momentum effect" – where previously outperforming companies continue to outperform – is observable over shorter time frames (up to one year); however, consistent with financial literature, we find that this effect disappears on longer time horizons.[4]

As Giuseppe Tomasi di Lampedusa famously wrote in *The Leopard*, "If we want things to stay as they are, things will have to change." Our findings suggest that in order to maintain outperformance, companies should pursue preemptive transformation rather than relying on performance momentum to sustain itself.

Furthermore, the preemption premium is continuous: the higher the relative performance of a company when it initiates change, the higher its long-term relative performance. In other words, the earlier a transformation is initiated, the better (see Figure 1.2).

In spite of this pattern, preemptive transformations are uncommon. In a given year, only 15% of outperforming companies embark on transformation, while 20% of underperforming and 25% of severely underperforming companies (the bottom decile of firm performance) do.

There are exceptions. When Jack Ma founded Alibaba in 1999, internet penetration in China was less than 1%. Growth in that area was expected, but no one could predict its precise course. So, early on, Alibaba took an experimental approach, in which leaders constantly reevaluated their vision and, when necessary, restructured the company accordingly.

By 2011, Alibaba's online marketplace Taobao had captured more than 80% of the digital Chinese consumer market. Even though Taobao was highly successful, Alibaba decided to split it into three independent businesses[5] in order to participate in three possible futures for e-commerce: one for consumer-to-consumer transactions (Taobao), one for business-to-consumer transactions (Tmall), and one for product search (Etao). The restructuring resulted in two successful mass-market businesses and one strong niche market.

---

4 We find the correlation between past TSR and future TSR to be positive and statistically significant on a 6- to 12-month horizon, but approximately zero and nonsignificant on an 18-month horizon or longer. See also Damodaran and Aswath, *Investment Valuation: Tools and Techniques for Determining the Value of Any Asset,* 2012.

5 Martin Reeves, Ming Zeng and Amin Venjara, "The Self-Tuning Enterprise," *Harvard Business Review,* June 2015. https://hbr.org/2015/06/the-self-tuning-enterprise [accessed 9/5/2020].

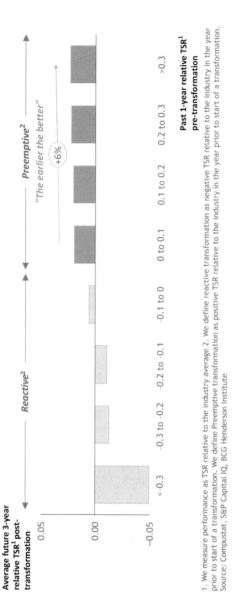

Figure 1.2: The Earlier a Company Transforms, the Better Its Future Performance.

Alibaba frequently reshuffles its more than 20 business units, so Taobao is just one example of many preemptive restructurings implemented as Alibaba grew from an 18-employee startup into a Fortune Global 500 company in less than 20 years.

Secondary Benefits of Preemption

In addition to having better financial performance, preemptive transformations offer three secondary benefits (see Figure 1.3). First, they take less time: pre-emptive transformations result in consecutive restructuring costs for an average of only 12 months, compared with 14 months for reactive ones. Second (and perhaps partly because of the shorter duration), they are less costly. The costs of restructuring in preemptive transformations total 1.5% of yearly revenues, on average, compared with 1.8% for reactive transformations.[6] Considering that these costs are only a proxy for the total transformation costs (which typically involve other expenditures, such as investment in new capabilities, M&A, and repurposing of assets), the real effect may be even larger.

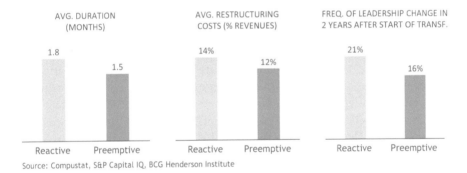

Source: Compustat, S&P Capital IQ, BCG Henderson Institute

Figure 1.3: Preemptive Transformation Takes Less Time, Costs Less, and Increases Leadership Stability.

---

6 Based on the sum of restructuring costs from the beginning to the end of the transformation effort (the end is defined as two consecutive quarters without restructuring costs).

By combining the lower average cost with the superior returns, we estimate the return on investment (ROI) of preemptive transformation to be approximately 50% higher than that of reactive transformations.[7]

Finally, preemptive change is associated with increased leadership stability. The share of companies experiencing a CEO change in the two years following the start of the transformation is significantly lower in the case of preemption (16% versus 21%).

Preemption as the Primary Success Factor in Transformation

How can leaders successfully implement preemptive transformation? Previously, we found several factors that can boost the odds of success:[8]

- *R&D spending*: Spending more on R&D than industry peers leads to a +5.1% increase in TSR versus underspending. However, there is limited value in heavily outspending peers, as this effect levels off rapidly.
- *Capital expenditure*: Companies with capital expenditure higher than their industry peers perform moderately better. However, the size of this impact is a third that of the R&D effect, probably because capital expenditure tries to improve existing models instead of exploring new growth models.
- *Long-term orientation*: Companies that are strategically more long-term oriented (based on analysis of their strategic language by a natural language-processing algorithm) outperform their peers by 4.8% TSR. This effect size increases to 7% in turbulent environments.
- *Leadership change*: Starting the transformation with a new CEO increases TSR by 9.2% versus 4.6% with an incumbent CEO over a five-year period, but with a short-run TSR dip of −3.9% in the first year. Turnover in the broader leadership team also matters; companies with more than 20% turnover in their leadership team have a 4.4% higher TSR over five years.
- *Large, formal transformation initiatives*: Publicly announced transformation initiatives have a positive effect on TSR, an effect that is exacerbated if restructuring costs are sizeable (>2% of revenue) and if the programs run for multiple years.

---

7 Based on the median estimated ROI of reactive and preemptive transformation, where ROI = ((change in dividend-adjusted market cap) − restructuring costs)/(restructuring costs).

8 Martin Reeves, Lars Fæste, Kevin Whitaker, and Fabien Hassan, "The Truth About Corporate Transformation." *MIT Sloan Management Review*, January 2018. https://sloanreview.mit.edu/article/the-truth-about-corporate-transformation [accessed 9/28/2020].

Our analysis confirms that these success factors also apply to preemptive transformations. But a more fundamental question is whether and how timing affects that recipe for success. To answer that question, we used *gradient boosting*, a machine-learning technique based on decision tree models that measures how well each factor discriminates between successful and unsuccessful transformation outcomes.[9] The results show that transforming preemptively as opposed to reactively is actually *the most important success factor* of the transformation – in other words, timing is the best predictor of success.

In preemptive transformations, R&D expenditure and capital expenditure are the next-most-decisive factors, reflecting a need to properly understand and invest in the future. In reactive transformations, leadership change is the second-most-important success factor – perhaps because companies that have already allowed performance to decline need to refresh their leadership and culture in order to accelerate change.

Microsoft illustrates how preemptive transformation with heavy investment in the future allows a company to sustain performance. After a few years of stagnating performance in 2009–2012, the software company managed to create strong momentum in 2012–2014 (36% annualized TSR). Rather than resting on its success, Microsoft changed its CEO and restructured again preemptively in 2014, which enabled it to preserve its momentum and continue to strongly outperform. The transformation aimed to orient the company to the new dominance of mobile and cloud,[10] even though these trends had not yet damaged the bottom line. In March 2018, Microsoft announced yet another restructuring amid strong performance.[11] For the first time, Microsoft will not have a division devoted to personal computer operating systems. Again, the company is trying to adapt preemptively to the ongoing technology changes and an evolving competitive environment.

---

9 Based on an extreme gradient boosting (XGBoost) algorithm. Gradient boosting algorithms create a decision tree–like structure, where the hierarchy of nodes gives the relative importance of attributes for outcome prediction, and iteratively refines the tree structure based on "error correction" between observed data and modeled values. See Chen and Guestrin, "XGBoost: A Scalable Tree Boosting System," *22nd ACM SIGKDD International Conference*, 2016.

10 Simon Bamberger, Wolfgang Bock, Patrick Forth, Anna Green, Derek Kennedy, Tim Nolan, and Neal Zuckerman, "Riding the Waves of Innovation in the Technology Industry," *BCG Publications*, October 27, 2016. https://www.bcg.com/publications/2016/hardware-software-entertainment-media-riding-waves-innovation-technology-industry [accessed 9/5/2020].

11 Don Reisinger, "Microsoft Is About to Undergo a Major Reorganization: Here's How It Breaks Down," *Fortune*, March 29, 2018. https://fortune.com/2018/03/29/microsoft-reorganization-terry-myerson/ [accessed 9/5/2020].

Six Steps to Successful Preemptive Change

Faced with a need to adapt to changes in their business, technology, or competitive environment, companies should transform early, before financial performance has started to decline. How can leaders turn around the successful company?

1. **Constantly explore.** To be able to transform preemptively, leaders need to anticipate change by continually exploring new options. The observation of biological systems[12] teaches us that it is optimal for companies to begin searching well before they exhaust their current sources of profit, and that firms should use a mix of "big steps" to move to uncharted terrain and "small steps" to uncover adjacent options at low cost. This requires balancing short-term tactical moves with a long-term aspiration, and investing enough in the future, especially in digital technology and R&D.

2. **Create a sense of urgency.** When a company is doing well, danger lies in self-satisfaction. Leaders shouldn't wait for an actual crisis to mobilize. Creating a sense of urgency[13] is the best way for leaders to preempt the risk of complacency. Using alternate scenarios, studying maverick challengers, surveying dissatisfied customers or noncustomers, and other exercises can help management envision new risks and opportunities, and test the resilience and adaptability of the current business model in a changing environment.

3. **Watch out for early-warning signals.** Most financial metrics, such as earnings, profits, or cash flow, are backward looking. Detecting the need for change requires a variety of early-warning signals for phenomena that have not yet affected the bottom line. Forward-looking metrics such as vitality[14] can help assess a company's readiness for the future.

4. **Create transformation capabilities.** Moving quickly against risks and opportunities is essential. This requires building permanent transformation capabilities and strengthening the adaptability of the organization. In particular, leadership teams should balance the right mix of fresh ideas and

---

12 Martin Reeves, Simon Levin, and Kevin Whitaker, "Leaping Before the Platform Burns: The Increasing Necessity of Preemptive Innovation," *BCG Publications*, April 25, 2018. https://www.bcg.com/publications/2018/leaping-before-platform-burns-increasing-necessity-preemptive-innovation [accessed 9/5/2020].

13 Martin Reeves, Ryoji Kimura, and Rodolphe Charme di Carlo, "Creating Urgency amid Comfort," *BCG Publications*, February 16, 2018. https://www.bcg.com/publications/2018/creating-urgency-amid-comfort [accessed 9/5/2020].

14 Martin Reeves, Gerry Hansell, Fabien Hassan, and Benjamin Chan, "Measuring and Managing Corporate Vitality," *BCG Publications*, October 19, 2017. https://www.bcg.com/publications/2017/strategy-strategic-planning-measuring-managing-corporate-vitality [accessed 9/5/2020].

experience to foster innovation[15] and ensure that new ideas are constantly explored and entertained.

5. **Control the narrative.** Preemptive change may generate frictions with stakeholders who believe that prudence and continuity are the best policies. Leaders should take control of the investor narrative and actively manage investor expectations in order to make preemptive transformation feasible. Defining and conveying the purpose of the company, and relating change efforts to that purpose, can also help energize and recruit employees and middle management for change efforts, which may otherwise be perceived as threatening (see Chapter 6). Indeed, a reliance on reactive approaches has caused transformation to become associated with painful, defensive, and remedial change efforts, whereas preemptive transformation is more likely to be focused on innovation and growth from the outset.

6. **Choose the right approaches to change.** Companies tend to drive change with a monolithic, linear project-management mindset. But there is no universal form of change. In reality, a complex business transformation comprises multiple types of change.[16] Each form requires a different mindset and different change management mechanisms. While the transformation may be run as a comprehensive program under a consolidated agenda, leaders should de-average and sequence the different forms of change. In particular, preemptive change is more likely to rely on adaptive or visionary models of change, rather than heavy-handed, top-down approaches.

Preemptive change is challenging for leaders to deliver, as they need to galvanize the organization for change without a clear external threat. However, reactive change driven by external threats is even harder to execute successfully. The next six chapters detail the steps you can take to increase the chance of success of your preemptive transformation.

---

15 Rocío Lorenzo, Nicole Voigt, Miki Tsusaka, Matt Krentz, and Katie Abouzahr, "How Diverse Leadership Teams Boost Innovation," *BCG Publications*, January 23, 2018. https://www.bcg.com/publications/2018/how-diverse-leadership-teams-boost-innovation [accessed 9/5/2020].

16 Martin Reeves, Simon Levin, Jack Fuller and Fabien Hassan, "Your Change Needs a Strategy," *BCG Henderson Institute*, May 17, 2018. https://bcghendersoninstitute.com/your-change-needs-a-strategy-2510061f51a9 [accessed 9/5/2020].

Martin Reeves and Simon Levin

Chapter 2
Think Biologically: Messy Management for a Complex World

When Soviet premier Nikita Khrushchev barked, "We will bury you!" in 1956, it was not considered an empty threat. It was seen as a real existential threat to capitalism and the American way of life. Many Western intellectuals believed that planned economies might indeed outperform free markets, whose inherent shortcomings – such as volatile economic cycles, lower investment rates, and the inefficiencies of competition – put capitalism at a relative disadvantage.[1]

Of course, reality turned out very differently, and we can see clearly today why planned economies almost invariably fail. They suppress diversity, initiative, innovation, and the adaptive capacity necessary for survival in an unpredictable environment. This lesson from history reveals an important insight: not only are there inherent limits to human intervention in a complex system – such as the economy – but we have difficulty seeing those limits before the fact.

The same lesson applies to businesses operating in today's rapidly changing and unpredictable global environment. We have argued that businesses, like forests or oceans or ant colonies, are complex adaptive systems (CASs), in which local behaviors and events can cascade and reshape the entire system.[2] As such, businesses are neither fully controllable nor predictable. Traditional approaches to management, which presume the opposite, are therefore often inadequate to address current business challenges.

To succeed over the long run, business leaders must not rely only on the traditional "mechanical" approach to management, which seeks to direct a company toward desired outcomes by engineering processes and controlling the behavior of its various components. They must also learn a "biological" approach, which acknowledges the uncertainty and complexity of business problems and so addresses them indirectly.

---

1 For example, the economist Peter Wiles argued that the Soviet economy had enough structural advantages over market-based economies that it was likely to outgrow them in the long run (see "The Soviet Economy Outpaces the West," *Foreign Affairs*, July 1953).

2 M. Reeves, S. Levin, and D. Ueda, "The Biology of Corporate Survival," *Harvard Business Review*, January–February, 2016.

https://doi.org/10.1515/9783110697834-002

Business as a Complex Adaptive System

In a complex adaptive system (CAS), local events and interactions among heterogeneous agents (in the business context, employees and units) cascade and reshape the entire system in a process called emergence. Those agents then respond to the system's new structure in a feedback process that drives further changes to the system. The system continually evolves in hard-to-predict ways through this ongoing cycle of emergence and feedback.

To see how this dynamic applies to businesses, consider corporate culture. Culture is an outcome of the behaviors and interactions of employees – their actions and words, and the way they treat one another – rather than what leaders and managers declare it to be. Executives are able to influence culture only indirectly by setting an example, providing incentives, and selecting and amplifying the right behaviors. Unlike factory production, which can be engineered and scaled up or down through hierarchical directives, culture cannot be directly controlled by managers.

For example, companies with a culture hostile to diversity have difficulty changing it precisely because this hostility usually arises not from a single controllable source but from the implicit assumptions, expectations, and behaviors of all employees. Plausible direct interventions such as compulsory diversity training and affirmative action programs tend to be ineffective – some research has shown that they can even retard progress. These top-down initiatives tend to fail because rules and compulsion frustrate employees' need for autonomy and provoke negative reactions that undermine the attainment of the initial goal. The dynamics of complex systems can thus cripple mechanical interventions.

Traditional Managerial Approaches Fall Short

There is for sure a growing understanding of the importance of complexity in business. Nevertheless, managerial instinct is still often mechanical and deterministic: managers instinctively prioritize predictable business problems and look for ways to "engineer" solutions to them. As a result, planning and optimizing are still the dominant paradigms of business strategy. For example, many CEOs and boards of directors view their objective as increasing total shareholder return (TSR), and they aim to do so through direct and controllable measures such as financial engineering and cost cutting. But making TSR an explicit priority and pulling the obvious levers of value creation can actually be counterproductive.

A case in point is Valeant Pharmaceuticals. Valeant's strategy to drive shareholder value was to pull the levers that would increase profits in a direct and predictable fashion. For example, Valeant took advantage of lower tax rates abroad, tightly managed costs, and raised prices aggressively. It also minimized spending on R&D, preferring instead to acquire drugs developed elsewhere. These levers had an immediate positive effect on Valeant's bottom line – indeed, Valeant was one of the best-performing pharmaceutical companies in the early 2010s. However, they ultimately impoverished Valeant's long-term growth opportunities and alienated stakeholders in the broader ecosystem. The direct cause of Valeant's collapse, in which the company lost more than 95% of shareholder value, was an alleged accounting fraud involving a specialty pharmacy booking fake sales. However, the more fundamental problem was that the mechanical pursuit of TSR growth did not actually create sustainable long-term value. Valeant is now under new management and has adopted a very different management philosophy, with a mission stressing patient health, a more prudent pricing and access strategy, and increased investment in R&D.

Although a mechanical approach works well in situations with high stability and low complexity, such as a production factory, it has a number of characteristics that make it ill-suited to CASs. For instance, it assumes linear interactions and straightforward cause-and-effect relationships while ignoring higher-order effects, and it suppresses adaptive learning by minimizing tinkering and deviations from prescribed processes. Mechanical management is becoming less and less effective in today's business conditions, in which global competition and rapidly advancing technologies make both companies and their business environments more complex and less predictable.

Balancing the Mechanical and the Biological

How should managers strike the right balance between the mechanical and the biological? It's helpful to think of the two approaches as different bands in the electromagnetic spectrum. We are used to looking at the world through visible light. But it's not that x-ray, infrared, and UV spectra are "wrong" or that the visible spectrum is "right" – they provide different ways of looking at the world, and they are each appropriate in different circumstances. We understand the world best when we know when to apply each perspective.

As companies and the environment both become more complex, managers will increasingly need a meta-management skill: the ability to understand the appropriate approach given the particulars of a situation. Applying the wrong managerial approach can negate the value of good thinking and execution downstream.

Here is a heuristic: biological management is most useful under conditions of high unpredictability and high complexity. These conditions are characterized by numerous and heterogeneous agents, nonlinear interactions, rapid cycles of emergence and feedback, and a high degree of co-evolution between business and the environment. Innovation and new business development are examples of activities that may benefit from biological management. It's impossible to know before the fact which combination of people produces the best outcomes or what products best fit the market; managers should seek to *create* variance, tinker, and continue to receive feedback from the market until they find success.

Mechanical management is most suitable for relatively stable and predictable environments. In departments like accounting, payroll, and legal, for example, traditional managerial approaches such as process optimization and efficiency maximization work well. In addition, environments that a manager can control precisely – a factory that has limited interactions with outside stakeholders, for instance – tend to reward mechanical management. It is for this reason that planning, process design, and lean methods all pay dividends in manufacturing. Ultimately, sound management must find the right mix between mechanistic and biological, adaptive thinking.

Toward Biological Management

Pointing out the flaws of traditional management is not enough. Businesses need a pragmatic alternative. Instead of focusing just on the parts of businesses that are easily intelligible and predictable, leaders should start by acknowledging the inherent complexity of running businesses and taking the implications seriously.

To "manage" complex adaptive systems, companies must overcome several fundamental challenges. First, they must be able to understand and exploit the link between local behaviors and macro-outcomes and use the right leverage points to allow global change to emerge from local actions. Next, they must manage the conflict of interest between the system's multiple levels. In addition, they must be able to maintain robustness in a changing environment as well as avoid being pulled into unfavorable basins of attraction (that is, conditions that are difficult to escape). Finally, companies must adjust their approaches in response to changing circumstances.

We propose six practices that address these challenges. Taken together, they constitute a biological approach to management. The practices apply as much to businesses as they do to other complex adaptive systems, such as fisheries and cities.

1. **Understand and exploit the link between local behaviors and macro-outcomes.** It is no surprise that the process of emergence in a complex adaptive system cannot be described precisely. It is for this reason that the outcomes of these systems are nearly impossible to predict – and that the mechanical management of them is therefore often unwise. For instance, no degree of micromanagement of researchers' behaviors can guarantee higher productivity in R&D departments. Controlling lower-level processes, no matter how precisely, cannot guarantee innovation.

   Nevertheless, this does not imply that there are no useful links to be exploited between local behaviors and macro-outcomes. Rather, it implies that business leaders should look for these links using the right statistical approaches. For example, although we cannot predict the weather in New York a year from now – even if we have the most accurate meteorological measurements possible – we can still be confident that we should bring a coat if we are going there in January. Likewise, venture capitalists and startup accelerators know that they cannot predict the success of particular companies they fund; instead, they seek to take advantage of the law of large numbers by managing a portfolio of numerous bets.[3]

   Another important business example of such a link between macro and micro scales is the experience curve, which connects the cumulative production of a good with its unit cost of production. Typically, each time cumulative volume doubles, the unit cost of producing a good decreases by 20% to 30%.[4] This idea was developed not through deductive reasoning about labor efficiency and process design; rather, it was a purely empirical observation. Whatever the reason, experience led to lower costs. The idea had a profound impact on business strategy: it meant that market share leadership could be decisive since the associated cost advantage could be self-perpetuating. The idea of the experience curve proves that managers can profitably understand and exploit the links between micro and macro

---

3 The law of large numbers states that the sample average approaches the expected value over a large number of trials. For venture capital firms, a large number of investments can make their overall payoff more predictable.

4 See M. Reeves, G. Stalk, and F. Scognamiglio, "BCG Classics Revisited: The Experience Curve," *Boston Consulting Group Publications*, May 2013.

behaviors, even in complex systems, in which the mechanism underlying these links is opaque.

How can business managers learn to identify such links? First, they should use the correct tools. Agent-based modeling and other local interaction models, for instance, can produce rich insights about how behaviors propagate and how small changes can have a large impact. Second, business managers should learn to look at their problems through a statistical lens. As is true of the climate, venture investment outcomes, and the experience curve, most of what we can say about complex systems is statistical and inductive rather than deterministic.

2. **Find and use the right leverage point in the system.** In systems without complexity, such as a mechanical watch, the point of highest influence is usually clear; changes propagate predictably from the beginning of a causal chain. In complex adaptive systems, the right approach for intervention is rarely obvious because of feedback loops, nonlinear relationships, and nonobvious cause-and-effect relationships. For example, the reintroduction of wolves into Yellowstone National Park set off a cascade of ecological changes – not only increasing the ecosystem's diversity but also restoring willow and aspen populations, thereby stabilizing riverbanks and modifying river flow. Surprises and unpredictable outcomes are the norm when intervening in a complex system.

How, then, should executives think about interventions in complex businesses? They should start by tinkering with varying degrees of directness. Business interventions exist on a spectrum of very direct to very indirect; the right level can be discovered only through experimentation. Take again, for example, the challenge of enhancing corporate diversity. The most direct intervention might be to set a hiring quota. However, there are many other less direct approaches: from shifting the pool of candidates, to addressing inherent bias in HR processes, to reducing the role of subjective judgment, to redefining the concept of diversity. Typically, indirect interventions – those that change the mindset, context, and assumptions informing particular actions – prove to be more effective because they touch the deeper, more persistent drivers of behavior. Moreover, tinkering at multiple levels of directness generally beats pure deduction in identifying such measures.

Therefore, finding the right leverage point often requires expanding the scope of problem solving beyond the direct and obvious level. Consider, for example, how Intel came to dominate the microprocessor market by starting from the right leverage point. Before the 1990s, computers were defined by their brand, software, and specs – no one thought that the brand of a microprocessor made much difference. Intel's marketers naturally focused on their direct clients – the design engineers at computer manufacturers. Their challenge was that as the microprocessor market matured, microprocessors started to become commoditized and the adoption of new products slowed significantly. In 1989, Andy Grove, then chairman of Intel, let his technical assistant run a marketing experiment with a $500,000 budget: instead of marketing to design engineers, Intel would target consumers directly.[5] The positive result of this experiment led to the enormously successful "Intel Inside" campaign, which transformed Intel from an unknown component manufacturer to a household name and, in the process, helped increase Intel's value by more than 40 times in the 1990s. Intel found the right leverage point for growth by tinkering and experimenting with a less direct intervention.

3. **Manage conflicting interests between levels or agents.** A fundamental challenge of managing complex adaptive systems is that they often consist of multiple levels, whose interests can conflict. Employees, businesses, and the players in broader business ecosystems all have separate interests. Business leaders must strike an equitable balance between levels.

   To do so, they should follow two principles: first, they should establish mutualism, reciprocity, and fairness in the interactions among agents and between levels. For example, an ecosystem orchestrator should ensure that all participants receive an equitable share of the value the ecosystem creates. Second, they must make sure that the higher system levels provide real feedback to lower levels and allow for local adjustment and failure. Put simply, there must be mechanisms to amplify desirable outcomes and diminish undesirable ones.

   In human CASs, transparency and fairness of institutions make trust and collaboration possible. Elinor Ostrom, for example, studied the conditions under which fisheries are able to self-organize in order to avoid the Tragedy of the Commons (a situation in which stakeholders overexploit shared resources, to the detriment of everyone involved). Her conclusion was that trust, reciprocity, and transparency were some of the pillars of groups that successfully self-organize.[6]

   One of the surprising features of complex adaptive systems is that local failures are costly in the short run but essential for the viability of the larger

5 Y. Moon and C. Darwall, "Inside Intel Inside," *Harvard Business School Case*, June 2002.

6 Ostrom, Elinor. *Governing the Commons: The Evolution of Institutions for Collective Action.* Cambridge University Press, 1990.

system in the long run. In nature, periodic local forest fires temporarily harm ecosystem productivity but help avoid catastrophic fires that damage the ecosystem over a much longer timespan. There are clear analogues in business: companies that keep failing businesses alive can avoid short-term pain, but they ultimately lose vitality because of increasing complexity, loss of focus, and resource misallocation. The tension between CAS levels is never resolved if local failures are prevented.

The Japanese media company Recruit exemplifies how companies can grow sustainably by building healthy ecosystems. Recruit, one of the most successful large companies in Japan, had a compound annual growth rate (CAGR) of close to 20% from 2011 through 2016 in a sluggish economy. This growth has been driven by the cultivation of various ecosystems (in areas as diverse as tourism, dining, and used car sales) in which the company serves as an orchestrator, promoting the long-term success of multicompany ecosystems rather than just its own P&L.

For example, Recruit created an ecosystem of small businesses by offering an iPad-based POS (point-of-sale) system called AirREGI free of charge. Through AirREGI, small businesses are able to access outside service providers and developers in areas such as advertising, accounting, workforce management, procurement, payment processing, and even cutting-edge recommendation engines powered by machine learning. The initiative grew explosively, reaching a hundred thousand businesses in its first year, partly because Recruit was willing to postpone monetization in order to maximize the value of participating in the ecosystem. For instance, Recruit sacrificed some immediate profits by opening up the AirREGI ecosystem to third-party providers – even where it had its own competing services or the capability to build them. By doing so, Recruit not only promoted ecosystem health but also enhanced the vitality of its own teams by exposing them to external competition and collaboration.

4. **Maintain robustness in a changing environment.** One of the most important challenges in managing a large, complex business is making it robust in the face of shocks. In a complex adaptive system such as a business, which evolves constantly along with the environment, it is impossible to enumerate all possible sources of risk. Instead of addressing each individual risk, then, managers must instill heterogeneity, redundancy, and modularity – properties that enable systems to withstand and adapt to shocks.

The human immune system is an excellent example of a system with such properties: it has a diverse set of antibodies and responses to address myriad potential attacks, three layers of defense, and loose boundaries between levels, which confine infections to one part of the body. If any of these features were missing, people would not survive for long except in a sterile environment. These principles apply just as much to businesses. Moves such as building financial buffers, investing in diverse people and initiatives, and building in redundancy for critical functions all help ensure long-run survival.

These basic properties of robustness are important in complex adaptive systems because complexity can amplify the potential impact of shocks. Interactions within the system are nonlinear, so small perturbations can compound into large, destabilizing transitions as they are propagated throughout the system. The recent bankruptcy of Westinghouse is a case in point. The downfall stemmed directly from the acquisition of CB&I Stone & Webster, a nuclear construction contractor. The inherent complexity of the nuclear construction business amplified liabilities involved in the acquisition, which grew to more than $9 billion. The seemingly innocuous $229 million acquisition turned out to be an equivalent of betting the house. Westinghouse went bankrupt because it was not properly insulated – both its modularity and redundancy were compromised.

5. **Avoid unfavorable basins of attraction.** Complex systems often have configurations or situations toward which they move naturally. These so-called 'basins of attraction' can be favorable or unfavorable, but they have a reinforcing feedback cycle, so they cannot be escaped through small perturbations. CASs are therefore at risk of stagnation and collapse when they fall into an unfavorable basin.

In business, a prototypical unfavorable basin of attraction is the success trap, which successful companies can fall into when they focus on exploiting known, validated opportunities (their "success formula") and lose the ability to take risks, explore, and create new growth opportunities. Our research has shown that this is a measurable risk plaguing large, established companies – in fact, seven out of ten companies that fall into this trap fail to escape it in five years. Large companies are the most vulnerable because their momentum makes it difficult for them to take sharp turns. They can run into unfavorable basins even knowing that they lie ahead.

To stay out of unfavorable basins of attraction, companies must develop the habit of nurturing variety in behaviors and encouraging actions with unpredictable but potentially large payoffs. It is not enough to promote *tolerance* of failures – instead, companies should actively foster initiatives with a high likelihood of failure. Intrapreneurship programs, self-disruption units, and minimum failure rates are all rarely used but potentially effective ways to promote new innovation initiatives. Most businesses are entrenched in a mechanical worldview – managers want to be able to explain their endeavors, employees want to avoid failure, and investors want to see consistent returns – so they tend to tolerate insufficient variance. It requires an especially strong push toward risky initiatives to get companies out of the success trap.

Amazon, despite enormous size and success, continues to epitomize this approach. It starts from the top: Jeff Bezos, in his April 2016 letter to shareholders, declared that Amazon is "the best place in the world to fail." He explained that a company should take bets that are 90% likely to fail, as long as the potential payoffs are high enough. For example, Amazon Marketplace was an outcome of persistence after two successive failures – Auctions and zShops. The willingness to continue taking big swings despite strikeouts has allowed Amazon to hit home runs in many disparate areas, not just in online retail with Marketplace, Prime, and FBA, but in completely new endeavors such as AWS, Kindle, and Alexa.

6. **Adapt approaches in response to changing circumstances.** One of the traps of mechanical management is the tendency to seek universal and permanent solutions to complex problems. Processes and procedures are alluring, especially in large organizations, because they seem to be ways to tame complexity by dividing problems into simple tasks that can then be managed separately and predictably repeated. The problem is that the world is more complex than these static universal processes acknowledge – and even if they work for a while, they inevitably become stale and outdated as the environment changes.

   In a complex world, there is no universal formula for problem solving. So what should managers do? Their best bet is to iteratively conduct small, low-cost experiments that can then be scaled up or down on the basis of their relative success. Scott Cook, the founder of Intuit, emphasizes that teams should make decisions by running experiments quickly and cheaply, rather than basing them on intuition or authority.[7] Even Intuit's legal team operates this way, iteratively updating guidelines so the essentials can be expressed in plain English on a single page.

   This mode of problem solving through constant experimentation needs the right organizational enablers. Individual teams require the autonomy to run experiments with minimal hierarchical direction, because worthwhile ideas and initiatives often spring from individuals closest to the front line.

---

7 D. Baer, "Why Intuit Founder Scott Cook Wants You to Stop Listening to Your Boss," *Fast Company*, October 28, 2013.

Moreover, they need to be empowered to take full advantage of the experimental learnings. At Intuit, teams running experiments often have embedded data scientists to help them draw rigorous conclusions from their trials. Finally, teams require a culture that prioritizes learning over immediate profitability or efficiency. Experiments are not valuable unless there is a legitimate chance of failure, so businesses must help teams and individuals become bold enough to attempt such risky experiments.

Haier, the Chinese white goods giant, embodies this ethos of constant experimentation. Haier's philosopher-CEO Zhang Ruimin wanted an open, entrepreneurial, and continuously evolving organizational structure. His answer was to recast the entire company as an innovation platform for small, autonomous teams. Ruimin successively disintermediated and decentralized the company by transferring responsibility to small, self-managed units called zi zhu jing ying ti (ZZJYTs, or independent operating units). The company now consists of more than 2,000 ZZJYTs. These units are essentially autonomous experiments: they have their own P&L responsibility, and they must be validated by real, external customers and research partners in order to scale up.

The Importance of Biological Thinking

These interventions illustrate how biological management can work in practice. However, the crux of biological management is not the interventions themselves but the worldview upstream to them – something we call *biological thinking*.

Biological thinking matters for several important reasons: First, in complex adaptive systems, there is no single formula or framework that always works. In fact, the very defiance of formulaic problem solving is what makes CAS management so challenging initially. It's not possible to articulate before the fact how best to intervene in a given situation.

Second, actions that work in CASs do not make sense *except* in light of biological thinking. Mechanical management remains alluring precisely because it relies on a familiar and shared protocol for sense-making: it focuses on measurable outcomes such as efficiency and profitability; it makes initiatives easy to explain; and it gives managers a sense of control. Biological management stops being counterintuitive only when business leaders adopt a new managerial worldview.

Third, managing businesses successfully in today's environment involves new goals rather than just new problem-solving tools. In other words, businesses need a new *what* as well as a new *how*: for instance, surviving, in addition to winning; maximizing value for others, as well as for oneself; and prioritizing learning, as well as optimizing short-term performance. These new goals can be embraced only when businesses adopt biological thinking.

Therefore, instead of focusing on developing specific techniques or actions, managers should master the principles of biological thinking:

- *Pragmatism, rather than intellectualism:* In an old business joke, a strategist says of a new idea, "It might work in practice, but does it work in theory?" The reality is that managers also tend to want narratives and explanations. It is tempting to reject ideas that one cannot explain. Nevertheless, the lack of an obvious explanation does not imply that something does not work (or vice versa). Managers must acknowledge that things often work before we can explain why.
- *Resilience, rather than efficiency:* It's hard to argue against efficiency. What few managers recognize, though, is that it often trades off against resilience. Like excessive dieting, trimming too much fat can in fact be harmful to companies. The difficulty is that the benefits of efficiency are often immediate and visible, while its risks are latent and invisible. To balance the calculus, companies must make resilience an explicit priority.
- *Experimentation, rather than deduction.* Paul Graham once claimed that "the best startups almost have to start as side projects."[8] That's because when it comes to innovating, no one knows what will work. Great ideas, in particular, are often outliers that experts may have good reasons for rejecting. Biological management therefore demands getting your hands dirty and tinkering more often than it demands analyzing and theorizing.
- *Indirect, rather than direct, approaches:* In her influential analysis of system leverage points, Donella Meadows[9] pointed out that the most powerful leverage points in complex systems are all indirect, whereas the obvious leverage points like subsidies, taxes, and standards tend to be relatively ineffective. It's an idea that most business executives intuitively understand but hesitate to put into practice. Acting on structure, goals, mindset, and

---

8 Paul Graham, "Want to start a startup? Get funded by Y Combinator." http://www.paulgra ham.com/before.html?viewfullsite=1 [accessed 9/5/2020].

9 Donella Meadows, *Thinking in Systems: A Primer.* https://www.amazon.com/Thinking-Systems-Donella-H-Meadows-dp-1603580557/dp/1603580557/ref=mt_other?_encoding=UTF8&me=&qid= [accessed 9/5/2020].

other contextual drivers may seem unacceptably "soft," but these levers are often more effective than direct levers in the long run.

-   *Holism, rather than reductionism:* On the surface, reduction is a natural step in the problem-solving process. It makes problems more tractable and allows for division of labor. It works in engineerable systems, in which sub-components interact minimally or linearly. But reduction often fails in complex systems because the crux of their behavior lies in the relationship between parts rather than in the parts themselves. The whole is not the sum of its parts.
-   *Plurality, rather than universality:* Heterogeneity is the basic ingredient through which adaptation, and therefore renewal and growth, become possible. Innovation in cities scales superlinearly, not because their inhabitants are efficient and coordinated, but because their plural, competing viewpoints provide for constant growth and rejuvenation.[10] Likewise, companies can achieve vitality not through dogma or universal solutions but by nurturing plurality.

We have an innate need to understand and see simple, explainable patterns, even in a sea of complexity. But this desire can misguide us. Biological management is necessary because the world is not always orderly or easily explainable.

The biological approach makes management messy, iterative, and even counterintuitive and harder to articulate. Nevertheless, it is also a boon: it allows managers to tinker, to experiment, and to find solutions amid complexity. Biological management also draws on the initiative and diversity of people and liberates them from being mere instruments in mechanical processes – it is thus ultimately a more humanistic approach to management.

---

10 The process by which heterogeneous agents compete and renew the entire system is what the economist Joseph Schumpeter called "creative destruction."

Martin Reeves, Ryoji Kimura, and Rodolphe Charme di Carlo

Chapter 3
Creating Urgency Amid Comfort

Business success contains the seeds of its own destruction. Success breeds complacency.
Complacency breeds failure. — Andy Grove, Intel cofounder

By traditional performance metrics, large businesses are in a more comfortable position now than they have been for several decades, with record-level S&P 500 profits and cash balances (Figure 3.1). Economic conditions have been supportive, delivering broad-based growth across all major markets.

Available funds not invested[1], $B

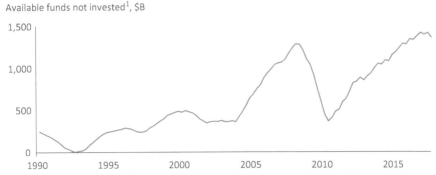

1. As defined on previous slide: free cash flows plus net debt addition and equity issuance minus private nonresidential investments
Note: Data on equity issuance not available before 2000, assumed to be the same as 2000 numbers (generous assumption since 2000 was peak of tech boom)
Source: Bureau of Economic analysis, Securities Industry and Financial Markets Association, BCG Center for Macroeconomics analysis

Figure 3.1: Large Businesses' Available Funds Are at Historical Highs.

Large businesses are capturing an increasing share of the pie, with revenues becoming increasingly concentrated in many industries. Firms have therefore been able to keep wages and investment levels low while simultaneously borrowing money at low interest rates.

Risks on the Horizon

Still, there are some plausible reasons for large businesses to be prudent and vigilant about how long the good times will last – at the level of the individual firm and the whole economy.

https://doi.org/10.1515/9783110697834-003

First, technological innovation continues at a dizzying pace. Incumbent enterprises continue to be disrupted by digital attackers, often from beyond familiar industry boundaries (Chapter 13). As a result, at the start of 2018, seven tech companies were among the top ten global firms by market capitalization (Apple, Google, Microsoft, Amazon, Facebook, Alibaba, Tencent), compared to one just a decade earlier.

This is only the visible tip of the iceberg. With *Fortune* magazine, we developed a ranking of the most vital US companies – those with the highest potential and capacity to grow in the long term. The Fortune Future 50[1] index shows the extent to which tech firms threaten traditional incumbents: the tech sector represents only 15% of the top US firms by revenue but 24% of today's fastest-growing companies and 64% of the Fortune Future 50.

Second, today's macroeconomic environment is fragile. Even as a cyclical recovery from the financial crisis continues around the globe, structural factors threaten global growth in the long run, as Christine Lagarde, head of the International Monetary Fund, opined at the 2018 meeting of the World Economic Forum in Davos.[2] In an era of secular stagnation, long-term growth rates have fallen across developed economies, and demographic trends will further constrain growth in the future.

Third, political and economic uncertainty has increased significantly. Income inequality is rising, while trust in business and government is falling, encouraging a populist backlash against two pillars of economic growth: global integration and technological progress. As a result, firms cannot take for granted that the favorable business environment will continue uninterrupted, and this could provide a further drag on performance.[3]

Finally, our research indicates that US companies' life expectancy is shrinking:[4] it has almost halved (-43%) since 1970, and the risk of disappearing – either by bankruptcy or through M&A moves – in five years has risen to more than 30% (Figure 3.2).

How to account for this trend in the context of rising profits and valuations? While the *performance* of large corporations might be high, their *vitality* – their

---

1 https://fortune.com/future-50/ [accessed 9/5/2020].

2 https://www.imf.org/en/News/Articles/2018/01/22/sp012218-opening-remarks-for-the-world -economic-outlook-update-press-conference [accessed 9/5/2020].

3 https://www.bcg.com/publications/2017/corporate-strategy-business-no-longer [accessed 9/5/2020].

4 https://www.bcg.com/en-us/publications/2015/strategy-die-another-day-what-leaders-can-do-about-the-shrinking-life-expectancy-of-corporations [accessed 9/5/2020].

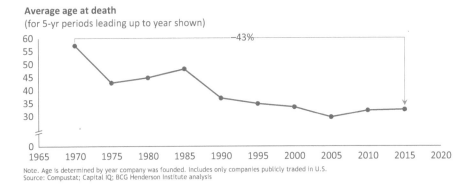

Figure 3.2: Life Expectancy of Companies Has Been Cut Almost in Half Since 1970.

capacity for growth and reinvention – is declining in many cases. According to our research,[5] large, established companies are increasingly vulnerable in this respect.

Today's executives are not blind to these risks. For instance, business model disruption and changing global economic conditions are among the top trends feared by business leaders.[6] However, the relative comfort of today's conditions might prevent their organizations from acting decisively to address these challenges.

Businesses Need to Avoid the Trap of Complacency

Companies are examples of complex adaptive systems, in which local events can have cascading effects on the entire system. In particular, complex systems[7] are susceptible to a sudden collapse, as demonstrated by many historical examples. This property is known as the Seneca Cliff,[8] referring to the Roman author who wrote, "Increases are of sluggish growth, but the way to ruin is rapid."

5 https://www.bcg.com/publications/2015/growth-innovation-tomorrow-never-dies-art-of-staying-on-top [accessed 9/5/2020].

6 https://www.nacdonline.org/analytics/survey.cfm?ItemNumber=66753 [accessed 9/5/2020].

7 https://www.bcg.com/publications/2017/think-biologically-messy-management-for-complex-world [accessed 9/5/2020].

8 http://thesenecatrap.blogspot.com/2015/11/the-seneca-effect-why-decline-is-faster.html [accessed 9/5/2020].

How can firms mitigate this risk? As Ugo Bardi, who coined the term, says, "If you want to avoid collapse, you need to embrace change, not fight it." But this cuts against the natural tendency to be complacent after success, rather than to keep questioning, challenging, and exploring. Complacency can blind leaders to new opportunities. Former Polaroid CEO Gary DiCamillo[9] explained Polaroid's denial of digital photography's potential, which doomed the firm to failure, by saying, "The reason we couldn't stop the engine was that instant film was the core of the financial model of this company."

A key challenge – and opportunity – for leaders today is to create a sense of urgency in their organizations, in spite of comfortable present conditions.

How to Create a Sense of Urgency Amid Comfort

There are several powerful ways in which leaders can create urgency under favorable conditions.

- *Conduct a maverick scan*: Disruption generally happens from the edges of an industry. There are usually many companies on the periphery of an industry that are taking bets against the business models of incumbents. Many will be startups, which are statistically unlikely to succeed, although their ideas might. But if it is hard for venture capitalists to judge which ones will break through, it is even harder for incumbents, who are likely to be wedded to their current business models. By inspecting these mavericks closely and asking, "What if their bet against our business model succeeds?" firms can create a sense of urgency and generate specific ideas on where to innovate and invest.
- *Survey "bad" customers*: Because current customers have already decided to buy a firm's products, surveying them often generates misleading positive responses, even in industries on the brink of disruption. To create a sense of urgency, it is sometimes more useful to survey noncustomers, defected customers, and dissatisfied customers. Posing the right questions also helps: asking about hopes, fears, and challenges might yield more information about future opportunities than asking about satisfaction with current offerings. And customers often are not explicitly aware of their unmet needs, so questionnaires must be supplemented by careful field observation. Most organizations are more willing to listen to a customer than

---

9 https://insights.som.yale.edu/insights/what-was-polaroid-thinking [accessed 9/5/2020].

to an internal change advocate, so outside-in signals are invaluable in creating a sense of urgency.

- *Construct stress scenarios*: It is hard for an organization to be successful if it does not believe in its current business model. However, it can also be fatal *not* to be paranoid about the vulnerability of one's current model and plans, especially in an environment where corporate life expectancy is declining. Firms can commit to their current plans while provoking urgency by thinking through the consequences of low-probability but high-impact competitive and environmental scenarios.

- *Conduct a "destroy your business" war game*: Jack Welch famously launched "destroy your business" exercises at GE during the e-commerce boom to mobilize his organization. By executing war games, in which one team defends and another attacks the current business model, leaders can vividly sensitize an organization to vulnerabilities and opportunities. And framing the exercise as a game legitimizes dissent and creative thinking, which may ordinarily be muted. Finally, the self-discovery of contingencies fosters deeper understanding and commitment than top-down analyses and pronouncements ever could.

- *Look at neighboring industries and geographies and ask why not?* A business model is not disrupted until it is, by which time it's usually too late to react. Similarly, skeptics of the need for change are correct until they are not. Organizations need to legitimize contingent thinking by entertaining counterfactuals – things that have not happened yet but *could* happen in the near future. Looking at disruptions in neighboring industries and geographies and asking *why not* is a powerful way to expand strategic thought and create an appropriate sense of urgency.

- *Map and eliminate frictions*: The above measures focus on reacting to emerging threats early enough to forestall them. But the surest way to avoid threats and shape the future is to *create* them. The Japanese word for crisis, *kiki*, means both danger *and* opportunity. Pioneers emphasize the latter. All industries exhibit "frictions," including distribution markups, contract complexity, and delays, which are often taken for granted. Pioneers can map and measure these frictions, innovating to proactively eliminate them before any customer or competitor has even thought about doing so. A sense of urgency is created by making visible to leaders what could be done – and thus what eventually will be done by a competitor, if they don't act first.

"Complacency is one of the risks we should go against," warned Lagarde at the World Economic Forum meeting in Davos.[10] We could not agree more, and we encourage business leaders to address this risk by embracing discomfort and creating a sense of urgency, precisely when it might seem least natural to do so.

---

10 https://www.euractiv.com/section/economy-jobs/news/imf-warns-of-harder-crisis-as-bullish-ceos-come-to-davos/ [accessed 9/5/2020].

Martin Reeves, Gerry Hansell, Kevin Whitaker, Tom Deegan, and Hen Lotan

Chapter 4
Achieving Vitality in Turbulent Times

Today's leading businesses are facing many near-term challenges in an uncertain economic and political environment. More than ever, though, they also need to focus on the long term, because the keys to success in the next decade will be different from today's.[1] Business leaders need to reinvent their companies for the future while ensuring strong performance in the present.

In other words, businesses need to maintain *vitality* – the capacity to reinvent the business and grow sustainably. To identify vital companies, as well as the factors that set them apart, we developed the Fortune Future 50[2] index in partnership with *Fortune* magazine. This year's index demonstrates that some companies remain vital in turbulent times – and points to how all leaders can make their organizations more vital.

The Vitality Imperative

Companies can create value in many ways, including pursuing efficiencies, streamlining assets, and raising investors' expectations; but in the long run, sustainable revenue growth is essential to value creation. Over periods of at least a decade, top-line growth accounts for three-quarters of the best-performing companies' total shareholder return.

Growth is becoming harder to achieve,[3] however, as long-run economic growth has declined (and is expected to continue declining as a result of demographic headwinds). And even for companies that grow rapidly for a short while, outperformance is increasingly difficult to sustain. As the pace of business accelerates and new models are exhausted more quickly, the speed at which the fastest-growing

---

1 Rich Lesser, Martin Reeves, Kevin Whitaker, and Rich Hutchinson, "A Leadership Agenda for the Next Decade," *BCG Publications*, December 14, 2018. https://www.bcg.com/publica tions/2018/winning-the-20s-leadership-agenda-for-next-decade [accessed 9/5/2020].
2 "The Fortune Future 50 2019," *Fortune*. https://fortune.com/future-50/ [accessed 9/5/2020].
3 Hans-Paul Bürkner, Martin Reeves, Hen Lotan, and Kevin Whitaker, "A Bad Time to Be Average," *BCG Publications*, July 22, 2019. https://www.bcg.com/publications/2019/bad-time-to-be-average [accessed 9/5/2020].

https://doi.org/10.1515/9783110697834-004

companies fade to the average has doubled in the past three decades. Past performance is less and less a predictor of future success.

To sustainably thrive, businesses need to build capacities for continual innovation and reinvention. This is especially difficult for large, established companies: complexity and inertia build as businesses age and grow, inhibiting the ability to drive change and renew advantage. Compounding the challenge, the most commonly used metrics for business (such as growth, market share, and profitability) measure only what *has* happened – which is no longer a strong indicator of what *will* happen. To look forward, leaders need to measure, and manage, vitality.

Vitality in Adversity

It may seem naive to focus on the long term given the adverse conditions that businesses face today. Macroeconomic signals are deteriorating; policy uncertainty has reached all-time highs; digital leaders are facing a backlash against technology; investors are becoming more skeptical; and there is widespread concern about the environmental and social externalities created by business.

There is still plenty of opportunity to grow in times of adversity.[4] Our research shows that even during economic downturns, revenue growth (not cost cutting) is the primary driver of financial outperformance, and companies that grow faster during downturns tend to continue growing faster after them. Additionally, companies that take a long-term perspective on strategy perform better than those focused narrowly on short-term issues. Finally, turbulent conditions are likely to increase competitive volatility – which means greater rewards for the companies that most effectively reinvent themselves.

For example, Amazon's market share in US e-commerce stagnated at roughly 5% from 2000 through 2006, more than a decade after the company's founding. But during the global financial crisis, Amazon maintained 25% annual growth even as the overall market slowed to a crawl, nearly doubling the company's market share in a three-year span. Amazon has continued to outgrow the market significantly every year since – demonstrating that even when the external outlook is difficult, vitality can pay long-term benefits, even for large, established companies.

---

4 Martin Reeves, David Rhodes, Christian Ketels, and Kevin Whitaker, "Advantage in Adversity: Winning the Next Downturn," *BCG Publications*, February 4, 2019. https://www.bcg.com/publi cations/2019/advantage-in-adversity-winning-next-downturn [accessed 9/5/2020].

The Drivers of Vitality

Our Fortune Future 50 index, now in its third year, aims to quantify the factors that contribute to corporate vitality and to identify the large global companies that are best positioned for growth. Vitality operates over long time periods, so it cannot necessarily be judged by short-term performance, but signs are positive so far: the companies from the 2017 and 2018 indexes have outperformed peers on both growth and TSR since publication (Figure 4.1). Innovation and growth are of course risky, and several individual companies have not lived up to their promise. Nevertheless, in aggregate, vitality today has been a good predictor of growth tomorrow.

The index incorporates factors demonstrated to predict long-run success, organized into five pillars: (1) market potential; (2) strategy; (3) technology and investment; (4) people; and (5) structure. It draws on nonfinancial factors as well as financial data. For example, we tested various ESG scores, recognizing that sustainability and social value are increasingly intertwined with long-term performance.[5] We consider gender diversity at several levels of the organization, finding (in line with prior research) that diverse companies are more innovative.[6] And we use natural language processing methods to decode strategic orientation from SEC filings and annual reports, identifying companies that take a long-term perspective, serve a broader purpose, and embrace uncertainty and complexity in their strategy.[7]

To survive the present and finance the future, especially in turbulent times, companies must also perform well enough in the present. Many of today's high-growth companies are losing significant amounts of cash,[8] in some cases triggering investors' fears – which may increase if economic conditions worsen. Therefore, we have excluded from our ranking companies that have negative cash flow from operations, an indication that any growth potential may be fragile. Additionally, we also stratify our list to account for companies facing other significant risks that could derail their ability to thrive in the future.

---

5 David Young, Wendy Woods, and Martin Reeves, "Optimize for Both Social and Business Value: Winning the '20s," *BCG Publications*, June 27, 2019. https://www.bcg.com/publica tions/2019/optimize-social-business-value [accessed 9/5/2020].

6 Miki Tsusaka, Matt Krentz, and Martin Reeves, "The Business Imperative of Diversity: Winning the '20s," *BCG Publications*, June 20, 2019. https://www.bcg.com/publications/2019/ winning-the-20s-business-imperative-of-diversity [accessed 9/5/2020].

7 Martin Reeves and Simon Levin, "Think Biologically: Messy Management for a Complex World," *BCG Publications*, July 18, 2017. https://www.bcg.com/publications/2017/think-biologically-messy-management-for-complex-world [accessed 9/5/2020].

8 Shawn Tully, "Fortune Analysis: The Tech Superstars Never Went Through Cash Like Today's Big Burners," *Fortune*, May 20, 2019. https://fortune.com/2019/05/20/fortune-analysis-the-tech-superstars-never-went-through-cash-like-todays-big-burners/ [accessed 9/5/2020].

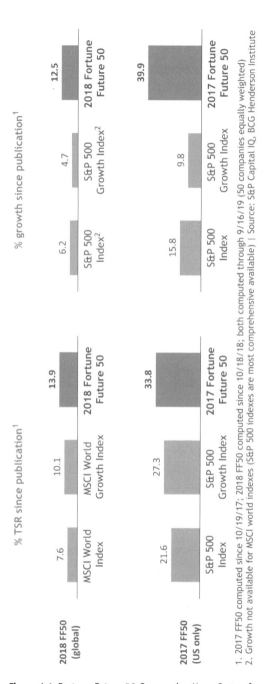

Figure 4.1: Fortune Future 50 Companies Have Outperformed Peers on Both Growth and TSR.

Patterns of the 2019 Fortune Future 50

The Fortune Future 50 index reveals a bipolar landscape: 88% of the 2019 index are located in the US or China (mainly in California and China's east coast). This distribution is in line with recent trends: more than 80% of the fastest-growing companies over the past three years also come from those two countries. Whereas 2018's ranking was split evenly between them, in 2019 the US accounts for a majority of the top 50, reflecting the differential in economic momentum.

When expanding more broadly to the top 200 companies, however, a wider range of regions is represented (Figure 4.2). Nevertheless, the patterns of vitality raise questions about the competitiveness of Europe in a bipolar technological world.

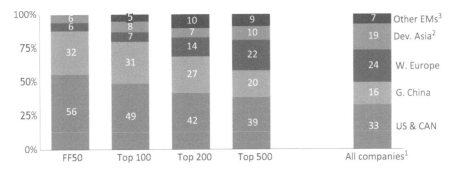

1. "All companies" global sample of 1,050 firms (companies with $10B+ sales or $20B+ market cap as of year-end 2018, excluding energy, metals & mining, commodity chemicals and REITs)2.Includes Japan, Korea, ANZ, Singapore 3. Includes India, Latam, Africa, Russia, SEA, Middle East | Sources: S&P Capital IQ; BCG Henderson Institute analysis.

Figure 4.2: Patterns in Company Vitality by Region.

A majority of the top 50 companies are in technology and communications services – and several others are digital natives (for example, Alibaba and Amazon in retailing). This may seem counterintuitive, given recent signs of investors' skepticism toward many tech companies and the emergence of a host of trust issues concerning technology. Indeed, the tech sector is coming of age, and beginning to face many of the regulatory and social issues of more mature industries – some companies may not survive the transition unscathed. But the index indicates that, beyond potential short-term fluctuations, tech capabilities are continuing to reshape business in the longer run. For example, even if the recent hype around some technologies turns out to be a bubble that deflates, the investments already made may still lay the groundwork for the next generation of breakthrough business models.

But despite the tech industry's prominence in the Fortune Future 50, the index displays a wide range of good and bad performance in every sector – only 10% of overall variation in vitality is explained by differences between sectors. One strong pattern in all industries is the negative correlation of vitality with age and size, reflecting the challenge of inertia and the necessity of reinvention (Figure 4.3).

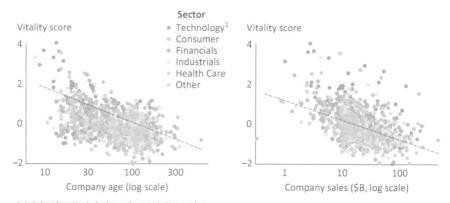

1. Includes information technology and communications services
Note: Shows global sample of 1,050 firms (companies with $10B+ sales or $20B+ market cap as of year-end 2018, excluding energy, metals & mining, commodity chemicals and REITs)
Source: BCG Henderson Institute analysis

Figure 4.3: Company Vitality Decreases with Age and Size.

Another pattern emerging from our index is that the most vital companies outperform on gender diversity, which is the dimension of diversity best captured by today's available data. One-quarter of executives at Fortune Future 50 companies are women, which is far from an aspiration of parity but significantly greater than the average of 17% for other large companies. Similarly, 18% of the top 50 companies have an executive team that is at least 40% female, a level reached by only 4% of their peers. These figures reflect the fact that diverse organizations are able to generate and harness a wider variety of ideas and are therefore better able to reinvent themselves for the future.

Finally, the index clearly indicates that the businesses with the greatest potential are not necessarily the ones with the highest performance today: of the companies with an above-average vitality score, exactly half are also above average in current performance (as measured by EBIT margin) and half are below (Figure 4.4). What it will take to succeed in the future is likely to be different

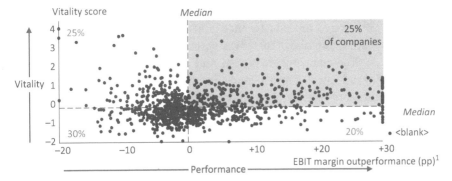

1. EBIT margin relative to sector median (outliers above 30% truncated for sake of display)
Source: S&P Capital IQ, BCG Henderson Institute analysis

Figure 4.4: Companies with an Above-Average Vitality Score May Not Have Above-Average Current Performance.

from what it takes to succeed today, so leaders need to both run and reinvent the business at the same time – what we call *ambidexterity*.[9]

How to Increase Vitality

Vitality is hard to maintain in large, established organizations, but the index points to some ways they can beat the odds:

- *Think differently about strategy*: It can be natural for leaders to focus on the day-to-day issues of running their business, but to maintain vitality, they need to counterbalance this tendency with a long-term, exploratory perspective. They must also recognize that traditional approaches to strategy and execution, based on deliberate planning and top-down direction, are often insufficient in today's business environment. Leaders instead need to master new strategic capabilities, such as *adapting* to shifts in the market, *shaping* the environment in which they operate, and *renewing* strategy when old models have been exhausted.

---

9 Martin Reeves, Gerry Hansell, and Rodolphe Charme di Carlo, "How Vital Companies Think, Act, and Thrive," *BCG Publications*, February 12, 2018. https://www.bcg.com/publications/2018/vital-companies-think-act-thrive [accessed 9/5/2020].

For example, graphics chipmaker Nvidia (number 26 of the 2019 Fortune Future 50) entered an industry that lacked a clear playbook; as cofounder Chris Malachowsky said, "There was no market in 1993, but we saw a wave coming."[10] The company envisioned and dominated a market for graphics processing units, which rose in tandem with the video gaming industry during the 2000s. More recently, the company saw an opportunity when the rise of deep learning brought new demand for GPUs. In response, Nvidia built platforms to shape the development of artificial intelligence chip technology with other tech leaders: the company partners with Amazon Web Services and Google Cloud to deliver machine learning infrastructure solutions, and it partners with automakers including Volkswagen, Mercedes-Benz, Toyota, and Volvo to develop autonomous vehicle technology.[11]

- *Build the right capabilities*: To deliver on their growth potential, businesses need to build a range of dynamic capabilities. These include technological excellence (even for companies that are not in traditional digital sectors), a diverse workforce with a culture that encourages the collision of ideas, and the organizational capacity to self-disrupt before being disrupted from the outside.

Visa (number 43) stands out as one of the oldest and most-established companies in the Fortune Future 50. It has maintained vitality in part by investing in a range of capabilities. To manage the transition to digital commerce, Visa has partnered with tech giants including Apple, Google, and Intel on payment apps and hardware, and it is internally investing heavily in AI for applications such as fraud prevention.[12] It also maintains diversity, with above-average gender diversity in its executive team and in the broader organization; and it has demonstrated resilience and adaptiveness over a long period, becoming one of the world's ten most-valuable public companies as of October 2019.

- *Organize for ambidexterity*: Vitality alone is not enough for incumbents to thrive sustainably; strong performance in the core business is also necessary in order to finance growth. However, running the business and reinventing it require different skills that are hard to balance – many companies fall into either the "success trap" (over-exploiting the current business, at the expense

---

10 Aaron Tilley, "The New Intel: How Nvidia Went From Powering Video Games To Revolutionizing Artificial Intelligence," *Forbes*, December 2016.

11 Johannes Hellstrom, "Nvidia boosts self-driving AI business with Volvo trucks deal," Reuters, June 2019.

12 Sara Castellanos, "Visa to Test Advanced AI to Prevent Fraud," *Wall Street Journal*, August 2019.

of tomorrow's) or the "perpetual search trap" (over-exploring, at the expense of profitable commercialization).

Leaders can find an equilibrium by structuring their organizations for *ambidexterity*. This can be done in four ways, depending on the diversity and dynamism of a company's environment: (1) *separating* segments of the business according to their situations, so that each can adopt a different approach to strategy; (2) *switching* strategic approaches over time; (3) *self-organizing* so that business units can choose a variety of approaches; and (4) tapping into *ecosystems* to benefit from partners that specialize in each approach (Figure 4.5).

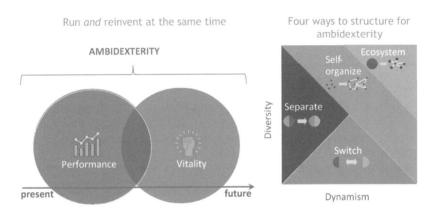

Figure 4.5: Structuring Organizations for Ambidexterity.

For example, Tencent (number 12) restructured its business in late 2018 for the first time in six years to align its organization with its strategic demands.[13] The company consolidated some business units in consumer-facing segments, which have historically driven its success; meanwhile, it created a division to focus on cloud computing, the industrial internet, and other business services it expects to be major growth drivers. By separating this group from its legacy businesses, Tencent can apply different strategic approaches to each part of the company.

- *Use forward-looking metrics*: Past performance is no longer as likely to persist, yet businesses today tend to be managed with only backward-looking metrics. Leaders need to complement those with forward-looking measures to understand their company's fitness for the future.

---

13 "Tencent announces a restructuring as challenges rise," *Reuters*, September 2018.

For example, Thornton Tomasetti, a leading engineering firm, has adopted methods to measure and manage its vitality.[14] The company monitors the share of its projects that incorporate recent innovations – an indicator of its capacity to develop new growth options – and it has taken actions to improve on key components of vitality, such as the number, diversity, and velocity of ideas in the organization. As chairman and CEO Tom Scarangello said, "We see vitality metrics as a way to quantify that we're doing what we need to do to achieve our goal of being the global driver of change and innovation in our industry."

Business leaders face many short-term issues, but the need to reinvent their companies for the long term is more urgent than ever. By emphasizing vitality, as well as current performance, companies can thrive sustainably.

How we Measure Corporate Vitality

The Fortune Future 50 index is based on two pillars. The first is *Future Market Potential* – the expectation of future growth from financial markets, defined as the present value of growth options (PVGO). This represents the share of a company's market capitalization that is not attributable to the earnings power of existing assets and business models. This pillar accounts for 30% of the index.

The second pillar is *Company Capacity* – our assessment of a company's ability to deliver on the future market potential. It comprises 19 factors drawn from a larger group of variables and calibrated against historical data for their ability to predict long-term revenue growth. This accounts for 70% of the index. These factors are grouped into four areas:

- *Strategy:* From 30,000 SEC filings and annual reports, we used a long short-term memory neural network (a natural language processing model that incorporates word order and context) to characterize a company's strategic orientation on three dimensions: (1) long-term orientation, (2) focus on a broader purpose beyond financial performance, and (3) "biological thinking." We also assess the company's clarity of strategy articulation from earnings calls and use the company's governance rating (according to Arabesque, a pioneer in ESG analytics).
- *Technology and Investment:* We assess the company's capital expenditures and R&D spending (as a percentage of sales, compared with sector averages); the growth of a company's patent portfolio (from a global database of patent filings) and that portfolio's digital intensity (the share of patents in computing and electronic communication areas); and the quality of the company's startup investment and acquisition portfolio (based on comparison with the best-performing global venture capital funds).
- *People:* We measure the gender diversity of the company's management and larger workforce; the age of its executives and directors; its leadership stability (represented by

---

14 "Annual Report 2018/2019: Vitality," *ThorntonTomasetti*, May 1, 2019. https://issuu.com/thorntontomasetti/docs/tt_annual_report_18-19 [accessed 9/5/2020].

the frequency of executive and director turnover); the geographic diversity of its directors; and the size of its board.

- *Structure:* We measure the age since company founding; size of the company (based on revenue); and growth track record (over prior three years and six months).

Companies were excluded from the Fortune Future 50 ranking if they had negative cash flow from operations over the prior three years on average, indicating elevated performance risk.

Jim Hemerling, Vikram Bhalla, Diana Dosik,
and Stephanie Hurder

Chapter 5
Building Capabilities for Transformation that Lasts

The CEO of a large consumer goods company was near the end of his rope. He was one year into a large-scale transformation that was focused on growth through a shift into premium products. The company had invested millions of dollars to develop an innovative product that warranted higher prices. The early results had been promising – initial sales were strong. However, the transformation was wrapping up, and the CEO's attention was being drawn to other challenges. The company had begun to revert to its old ways.

The engineering team did not seem to be on track to produce additional innovative designs. Recent prototypes were unimpressive. Discounting had crept back in, and the average price had fallen below the company's target. One successful product would not be enough to keep the business on track. Had the company invested millions to achieve only temporary results?

This predicament is all too familiar. Virtually all industries today face a whirlwind of new technologies, evolving customer behaviors, globalization, and pressure from investors. In response, companies launch transformations – profound changes to the company strategy, business model, organization, culture, people, and processes – aimed at achieving sustainable performance improvement.[1]

Yet many transformations fail to deliver. Why? In many cases, companies focus too much on the finish line and not enough on capabilities, the muscles they need to build and strengthen in order to get there and – most important – to stay there. By "capability," we mean an ingrained ability to do something well in a way that improves business performance. For example, a company could launch a transformation to improve its R&D performance, develop a new digital service, or change business models from wholesale to retail. Each of these transformations requires new, specific capabilities that the company needs to build – or acquire – to execute the transformation and sustain its benefits.

---

1 See "Transformation: The Imperative to Change," *BCG report*, November 2014; "The New CEO's Guide to Transformation," *BCG Focus*, May 2015; and "A Leader's Guide to "Always-On" Transformation," *BCG Focus*, November 2015.

https://doi.org/10.1515/9783110697834-005

Lasting transformations hinge on capabilities. Identifying and developing the requisite capabilities can mean the difference between a successful, sustained transformation and a short-term effort whose results quickly fade. In this chapter, we discuss the main reasons companies fall short in this regard, along with three imperatives for building capabilities effectively and generating lasting gains. Companies must address all aspects of the target capability by applying a comprehensive definition, following a systematic development approach, and making sure that the leaders are engaged and have committed their support.

Where do Companies go Wrong?

In many organizations, the approach to capabilities falls short for several reasons. First, as in the case of the CEO described above, some leaders fail to recognize the importance of the target capabilities and, therefore, do not think about systematically incorporating them into the transformation itself.

Second, building capabilities generally requires coordination across functions and business units. For example, developing a robust digital capability might require new talent (supported by HR), new tools (IT), new processes (operations), and new governance (leadership). In many companies, it can be difficult to bring these groups together in a coordinated effort and even harder to get them to see the big picture. As a result, many companies hand the capability-building process to HR alone or seek to address it through a few days of training.

Third, acquiring the new capabilities might represent a huge leap into the unknown. A company in a process-heavy industry such as mining might find it reasonably easy to develop lean capabilities to make its production processes more efficient. But it might struggle to implement a new digital capability that requires upgrades to employee skills, technology, and other aspects of the organization.

The biggest obstacle, however, is that new capabilities call for fundamental changes in behaviors – the ways that employees, managers, and executives work on a daily basis – and behavioral change is hard. Without a systematic and explicit approach, companies can, at best, change these behaviors only superficially and temporarily. Once the transformation process is over and attention shifts to the next priority, employees can easily revert to their old ways of working, and the improvements of the transformation disappear.

A Comprehensive Definition

To address these challenges, companies need to start with a comprehensive definition. As stated above, *a capability is a deeply ingrained ability to do something well in a way that improves business performance.* At the core are behaviors: the activities, interactions, and decisions made by a set of individuals in a company who exemplify that capability.

To enable and sustain such behaviors, we define four underlying components of a capability:

1. **Competencies:** The skills, knowledge, and beliefs held by employees
2. **Tools:** IT, databases, apps, and related systems
3. **Processes:** Activities, resources, and responsibilities that govern the way work is divided and done
4. **Governance.** Accountability, KPIs (key performance indicators), incentives, and reporting structures

Collectively, these four elements reinforce each other and lead to sustainable changes in behaviors, with the ultimate objective of helping the company create value (Figure 5.1).

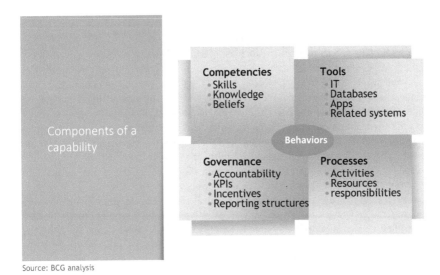

Source: BCG analysis

Figure 5.1: Components of a Capability for Creating Company Value.

Consider a consumer goods company that wants to build a capability in marketing and promotion. The company could change behaviors by systematically incorporating all four elements:

- Competencies could include, for example, knowledge about which promotions are best suited to specific retail channels, the analytical skills required to build a promotion strategy, and the belief that promotion decisions should be driven by data.
- Tools could include an analytics system that collects more accurate point-of-sale data, customers' mobile-browsing and purchasing history, and other information for generating insights for sales and marketing leaders.
- Processes could include the way the company plans for and rolls out events, how it allocates roles and resources across the team, and how field reps interact with store managers.
- Governance could include a new organizational function that reports to the CFO, new metrics to assess performance and improvement over time, and a new incentive structure for rewarding performance.

It's important to note that these elements are not always weighted equally. Certain capabilities emphasize some elements more than others. Nevertheless, a strong capability does incorporate some piece of all four elements in order to fundamentally reshape behaviors.

A Technology Company Builds a New Pricing Capability

Revenues and profits at a large office-product manufacturer were declining as the overall market for its products shrank. In response, the company launched a transformation to convert its business model: instead of selling products, it would sell services and solutions. As part of that transformation, the company set about improving and reshaping its pricing capability.

Prior to that point, pricing had been a cumbersome process that was linked to cost rather than to what the market would bear. Sales reps offered discounts that were based on gut instinct. And even in today's increasingly digital environment, the company had no pricing-analytics function: little sales data made it back out to the field.

In response, the company took steps to systematically build a pricing capability that was part of its transformation journey and focused on all four components:

- **Competencies.** Because pricing was such a critical element of the transformation – and because the company had had no dedicated pricing team prior to that point – leaders opted first to hire outsiders who already had the required competencies. The company created a new pricing and analytics group built around these experts. They trained company employees, rigorously developing their pricing knowledge, skills, and beliefs.
- **Tools.** The company developed an analytical tool that assessed product features and identified those with the biggest impact on pricing. In addition, the company rolled out a dashboard of sales data, which broke pricing down by region, product line, and sales rep. With these tools, the sales force gained a clearer indication of the pricing options for

specific customers, and analysts were better able to identify trends and support field reps. Management also used the tools to track performance.
- **Processes**. Several processes were altered, particularly those associated with discounting. Once a list price was set, sales reps had clear guidelines – and guardrails – regarding the discounts they could offer. Steeper discounts required approvals from higher levels – up to the global head of sales.
- **Governance**. The company created a new role: a vice president of pricing who oversees the entire function and reports to the CFO. The company also refined its performance incentives for the sales force, introducing a bonus scheme that emphasizes pricing and is simple enough that a rep can easily do the necessary calculations in his or her head.

As a result of the efforts associated with each of the four dimensions above, the behaviors of pricing team members have fundamentally changed. No longer do sales reps offer discounts on the basis of their gut instincts; instead, they have a standardized approach that is based on a quantitative analysis of the market. In addition, the company uses the pricing and analytics group to continually measure its performance and improve over time.

Within five months of rolling out the new capability, the company was able to raise prices by more than 2% on average, leading to approximately $50 million in new revenues – and an 8% improvement in gross margin – each year. As the transformation journey continues, the new pricing capability is helping the company ensure that these gains are sustainable.

Ten Key Practices for Systematically Building Capabilities

With a comprehensive definition in place, companies can turn their attention to identifying and developing the capabilities they will need to generate lasting change through transformation. On the basis of our experience, we have identified ten key practices for building capabilities (Figure 5.2 and discussed below).

1. **Ruthlessly prioritize the critical few capabilities that will deliver the greatest value.** The first step is to determine what is needed: the subset of capabilities that are critical for the transformation. This requires understanding the goals of the transformation and identifying the specific capabilities that will help the company achieve those aims. The company then needs to select the few capabilities that will generate the greatest value and prioritize ruthlessly. A company that tries to build too many capabilities at once can spread its resources too thin and accomplish nothing.

   For example, a consumer goods company sought to expand its global presence and to use digital technology to improve its performance. In support of these strategic objectives, the company conducted internal and external interviews and a benchmarking analysis and came up with a list of

1		Ruthlessly prioritize the critical few capabilities that will deliver the greatest value
2		Assess the gaps in all facts of the critical capabilities
3		Align leaders on the overall process
4		Design each capability, addressing all four components
5		Assemble a cross-functional team with the necessary expertise and perspectives
6		Use a rigorous change-management approach
7		Build capabilities in the context of employees' day-to-day work
8		Measure results and make course corrections
9		Address both the "hard" and "soft" aspects of the organization
10		Stay the course until the change becomes permanent

Source: BCG analysis

Figure 5.2: Ten Practices for Systematically Building Capabilities.

critical capabilities. To prioritize them, the company ranked the capabilities according to two dimensions: the relative importance of each capability to the company's strategy and the difficulty of implementation. Management decided that the capabilities that were important to the strategy and easy to implement would require relatively less direct oversight, which – later in the transformation – could be passed on to line managers. Conversely, capabilities that were important but hardest to implement would require a different approach. Those would require significant time, energy, resources, and commitment from leadership, so the company opted to create teams dedicated to building these as part of the transformation program.

2. **Assess the gaps in all facets of the critical capabilities.** Companies need to define the gaps between their current capabilities and their target state relative to all four components: competencies, tools, processes, and governance. Many companies err at this stage, thinking of capabilities as single-dimensional attributes rather than considering all four dimensions of each capability. The gap analysis helps organizations start to map out the effort that will be required during the transformation.

3. **Align leaders on the overall process.** Senior leaders at the company need to understand not only the target capabilities but also the full scope of the process required to develop them. Executives must be prepared to invest time and energy to see that process through. The process can extend over a long period during which the executives will likely face demands on their time and attention in overseeing the transformation itself. Clear alignment from the beginning offers a reality check for making sure that leaders are prepared to support the initiative.

4. **Design each capability, addressing all four components.** The next step is to design each of the required capabilities, addressing all four components of the definition. For example, a company seeking to build an R&D capability requires more than just technical expertise. It also needs, for example, tools to support research, processes to allocate resources among various projects, and metrics to evaluate performance. This requires recognizing that capabilities are not addressed only through training.

An Auto Manufacturer Builds Digital Capabilities

While some capabilities are unique to a specific company and transformation, others – such as digital technology – are more widespread and more complex to develop.[2] Digital encompasses singular, tactical capabilities such as big data, analytics, and social media, yet it also may require the company to make broader changes to its business model. Moreover, in many industries, it requires an influx of new talent through direct hiring, a joint venture, or a partnership with another company. More fundamentally, building a digital capability requires a new mindset of rapid prototyping and learning through experience.[3]

For example, the executives at a multinational automobile company recognized that it would need to incorporate digital technology more directly, both in its internal processes and in the vehicles it sold. The company launched a digital transformation, including a dedicated effort to build the components of their capabilities:

- *Competencies*: The company needed to develop several competencies, including rapid prototyping and analytics, to support digital capabilities. Management hired experienced outsiders and paired some of the new hires with current employees in a reverse-mentoring process that would spread competencies quickly throughout the company.
- *Tools*: The company upgraded its IT tools and systems across the board, making changes to more than 2,000 applications. For example, a new-product data-management tool allowed designers at multiple sites around the world to collaborate on new products and accurately track all information related to their development and release.
- *Processes*: Rather than using the traditional product-development approach, which is built on a linear series of steps, the company shifted to agile product development, which is faster, more iterative, and more focused on the customer experience. In an agile process, developers start by turning their ideas into a very stripped-down prototype, which they show to potential customers in order to capture their feedback. Using the agile approach, the company was able to deliver a full working version of a new product in just 13 weeks, during which there were several rounds of feedback and design changes from users. The process took far less time than would have been necessary using the old software-development approach.

---

2 See "The Digital Imperative," *BCG article*, March 2015.
3 See "How to Jump-Start a Digital Transformation," *BCG Focus*, September 2015. https://www.bcg.com/publications/2015/digital-transformation-how-to-jump-start-a-digital-transformation [accessed 9/5/2020].

- *Governance*: After a few early-stage tests, it became clear that the company didn't have the right internal IT structure in place to support the digital capabilities. It therefore split its IT function in two: one section would support the company's existing operations using traditional legacy systems, while the other would move faster to develop cloud-based mobile technology and other digital tools that could support the new initiatives.

Most important, employees, managers, and leaders all began to change their behaviors in lasting ways. For example, instead of interacting only occasionally, the IT teams made a habit of presenting the business teams with testable prototypes for feedback every two weeks. Procurement teams that had been spending three to six months recruiting vendors before offering long-term commitments started signing lower-risk trial-commitment contracts within one week.

As a result of these changes, the company was able to build digital features into its cars, giving drivers access to, for example, e-mail, voicemail, and entertainment features. It also was able to revamp its sales approach, incorporating the use of digital channels to reach out to customers at critical points in the car-buying process with highly targeted marketing messages, vehicle specifications, and other information intended to win them over. In the aggregate, the company estimated that with the incremental sales and reduced costs, the new digital capabilities would lead to approximately $150 million in profits in three years. Moreover, the company plans to continue to build on those gains.[4]

5. **Assemble a cross-functional team with the necessary expertise and perspectives.** During the design process, a cross-functional team can ensure that critical aspects don't fall through the cracks. Such teams include representatives from, for instance, HR, IT, and finance. The team does not need to be large, but it should include the right experts and stakeholders.

   The consumer goods company mentioned above created a permanent corporate function that is directly responsible for identifying and developing new capabilities and designing ways to embed them in the company. This function comprised people from HR, IT, and operations, as well as other departments.

6. **Use a rigorous change-management approach.** Creating lasting behavioral change is hard and requires the same rigorous approach to implementation as the transformation itself. A clear implementation plan built on rigorous change-management principles should include detailed milestones and KPIs, and it should establish the right team to execute the plan.[5]

---

4 For additional examples, see "How Five Companies Launched Digital Transformations," *BCG article*, September 2015.

5 See "Changing Change Management: A Blueprint That Takes Hold," *BCG report*, December 2012. https://www.bcg.com/publications/2012/change-management-postmerger-integration-changing-change-management [accessed 9/5/2020].

7. **Build capabilities in the context of employees' day-to-day work.** During a transformation, employees are under a great deal of pressure, and a seemingly-theoretical capabilities-building project is bound to raise skepticism. Rather than treating capabilities as an abstract exercise, companies need to make the capability-building experience as practical as possible, grounding it in employees' daily work and responsibilities. The goal of any transformation is to fundamentally change the behavior of employees and managers, leading to a new, permanent way of working. A capability-building program that is practical, based in the real work that employees perform daily, and executed in parallel to the business agenda of the change makes employees feel supported and leads to these real changes in behavior.

8. **Measure results and make course corrections.** Success requires measuring and reviewing the impact of all changes and adjusting the course as needed. The abstract nature of capabilities makes them challenging to define and assess. As such, companies need to establish quantitative goals and milestones, communicating openly and honestly with all involved.

To ensure the success of the overall program, implementation teams must use these metrics to continually evaluate and make appropriate adjustments.

An Industrial Company Pilot-Tests a Capability-Building Program for Managers

One industrial company had a culture that was highly oriented to processes and top-down directives. Rather than engaging in discussion and dialogue with their people, unit and department leaders acted like prescriptive taskmasters, and although the company posted decent returns, it had a poor track record for innovation. The company hired a new CEO who quickly realized that the culture was hindering the company's ability to solve complex problems. He initiated a transformation aimed at building up capabilities among frontline managers directly overseeing line employees. The goals were to reduce reliance on top-down tasks, increase dialogue between managers and their employees, and engage in value-based management that would ensure all managers and employees knew the potential financial impact of their decisions.

To develop these new capabilities, the organization, rejecting theoretical training programs, opted to address the work of the managers in practical and tangible ways. Managers were taught how to reframe daily conversations with their employees. The company restructured the morning meetings that line managers held with their units, allocating time for the active solicitation of employees' opinions and ideas, rather than simply issuing orders. Managers used simple tools such as checklists, feedback mechanisms, and learning guides to help them stick with the new target behaviors. After an initial pilot test, the company made some refinements and rolled out the program on a larger scale, training 6,000 line managers across 18 countries, in three languages.

With these new management capabilities in place, employees are now far more empowered to make suggestions, and managers have a much clearer sense of how to evaluate those suggestions. The teams – well-integrated units – are adding significant value. For example, a procedure for job sites that was recently implemented throughout the company and is saving roughly $400 million annually was the recommendation of a line employee.

9. **Address both the "hard" and "soft" aspects of the organization.** Once new capabilities are in place, companies need to take active steps to ensure those capabilities become embedded in the company's DNA. Such steps include changes to the hard elements of the company, such as IT systems, as well as softer aspects, such as performance assessments, incentives, and the overall culture.

   For example, a company that aims to have its sales force emphasize the quality of customer interactions rather than simply concentrating on upping the volume of sales calls would need to apply new metrics for evaluating customer interactions and to incorporate the new metrics into their performance-management system, including the award system. Furthermore, sales managers would have to emphasize the importance of high-quality customer interactions on an ongoing basis.

10. **Stay the course until the change becomes permanent.** There is no finish line, and the capability-building process is never over. Companies need to stay the course, reinforcing a particular initiative until the new behavior – no longer unfamiliar – becomes second nature for employees.

A Software Company Builds a Capability to Support a New Business Model

As customer preferences changed, a leading software and services company needed to transform its business model from on-premises licensed software to subscription-based, cloud-hosted software as a service (SaaS). That required developing several capabilities.

The company started in a few areas, analyzing customer expectations and benchmarking its performance against that of competitors to understand the biggest gaps. The most immediate priority was "customer success." Rather than selling software systems to customers on a one-off basis, the company had to interact with customers more frequently and directly, and it needed to develop a culture focused on anticipating and addressing their needs.

To build the customer success capability, the company assembled a cross-functional team with representatives from sales, service, and engineering. The team drew heavily on external benchmarking and expert interviews. These proved critically important, given that the company was expanding into an area in which it had little institutional expertise. Humility was key as well: even in designing the capability, leaders were leaping into unfamiliar territory.

On the competency front, the company built up its analytics and data-management skills, enabling it to track customer usage accurately and to synthesize the data into insights for improving products. It also rolled out dashboards that allowed the company to anticipate problems, spotting usage patterns, predicting customers' needs, and addressing needs rapidly.

With regard to processes, the company had to create value for its customers by building close, long-term relationships, thus improving retention rates. Finally, the company established a new role: a customer success manager serves as a single point of contact for handling all client needs. The company also altered its KPIs, focusing on adoption, retention, and customer-success metrics.

To embed the capability, the company redefined its target culture to emphasize customer service with specific behavioral changes. For example, it was no longer acceptable simply to pass customer problems from one department to another. Instead, because the company now aimed to resolve problems as soon as they arose, it authorized line employees to handle problems at the lowest possible level and collaborate to solve problems across functions.

Through these measures, the company has succeeded with the new SaaS business model, reducing churn among its customers and increasing revenues from upselling and cross-selling.

Implications for Leaders

Even companies that get the first aspects – a clear definition and the ten imperatives – right can fail if they lack the right leadership. Leaders need to guide the overall process, set expectations, model the new target behaviors, and use positive reinforcement to reward progress. They also need to allocate resources among multiple priorities and take other steps to support the change. All of this requires significant time and energy during a period in which those leaders are likely to be running other aspects of the transformation, as well as the day-to-day operations of the company.

To help leaders prioritize, we provide the following guidelines:

- *Know what you don't know:* Capability building can be especially difficult when the target capability resides outside the leadership team's expertise. Leaders are naturally drawn to areas they know well and to which they can quickly add value, but transformations don't always offer that luxury. For example, the leaders of a company that lacks first-hand digital experience but needs to become better at launching new digital initiatives might need to push themselves in ways that are unsettling. For this reason, it's critical that they understand their own limits and become creative and resilient in building capabilities. One approach is to rely on experts, perhaps hiring from companies that already have the required capabilities. Mentoring and coaching can help. And leaders should strip away the stigma and blame associated with failure, treating setbacks as opportunities for learning.

- *Balance medium-term capabilities with short-term business pressures:* Building capabilities takes time, resources, and energy. Moreover, the process can be thrown off track by the relentless pressure for short-term results and the competition for executive bandwidth and resources. Accordingly, it's up to the leadership to prioritize capabilities, allocate resources, monitor the overall workload of key employees, and link progress on capabilities to short-term results.

- *Prevent atrophy:* Organizational capabilities, like healthy muscles, atrophy if they are not tested, used, maintained, and improved. As we noted above, leaders must deal with a steady stream of new initiatives and priorities that can pull the company in new directions. To avoid losing ground, leaders must deliver strong, consistent messages about the importance of core capabilities, linking them to employee objectives and rewards and regularly evaluating capabilities against continually changing strategic requirements. Finally, leaders must foster a mindset that treats capability-building as an ongoing requirement rather than a one-time event.
- **Make the organization more agile**. Perhaps the biggest challenge for leaders, beyond developing individual capabilities, is anticipating the need to transform the company repeatedly over time. Even a theoretically perfect set of capabilities today will have to be revamped in the near future, so company leaders need to make their organization more agile, capable of thriving amid continual change.

The CEO we described at the beginning of this chapter eventually realized that focusing on the outcomes of the transformation wasn't enough. Members of the pricing team didn't simply need new products. They needed stronger pricing capabilities, including tools. Similarly, the R&D team needed new processes that were less cumbersome and more tightly linked to manufacturing. Broader scopes of responsibility would allow engineers to better integrate perspectives from developers, designers, marketers, and customers. In sum, by doubling down on the capabilities needed to execute the transformation, the company was able to grow through stronger sales in the premium segment and to generate sustainable gains.

Many companies that launch transformations focus doggedly on demonstrating outcomes. That approach is understandable, but because it doesn't address the underlying capabilities needed to achieve and sustain the outcomes, it's shortsighted and will likely fail. Regardless of industry or type of transformation, capabilities are critical elements in improving performance and sustaining results, ultimately in the form of increased value creation. By focusing on the three elements discussed here – a clear and robust definition of capabilities, a structured approach for building those capabilities, and the right support from leaders – companies can successfully transform themselves to meet whatever challenges they might face.

Ashley Grice, Martin Reeves, and Jack Fuller
Chapter 6
Getting Uncomfortable on Purpose

Thinking about purpose in business was once a provocative and urgent activity. A seminal *Harvard Business Review* article[1] from 1994 states, "In most corporations today, people no longer know – or even care – what or *why* their companies are," and argues that "strategies can engender strong, enduring emotional attachments only when they are embedded in a broader organizational purpose." At the time, purpose was a disruptive idea, reminding companies how disconnected they had become from their raison d'être and inspiring them to re-articulate it, recommit to it, and mobilize around it.

Yet like many new ideas in business, what starts out as a provocation can easily become an empty word, a comfortable routine, or even an excuse for *not* facing the toughest issues. Indeed, interest in purpose has surged, peaked, and declined, suggesting that the concept, like CSR, agile, and other initially powerful business ideas, has been overused and diluted (Figure 6.1).

A clear sign that purpose has lost its power is when the discussion becomes easy and comfortable – if in articulating purpose you are merely describing, rather than disrupting, how your company works. Such discussions are probably not adding much value. Yet the reasons for a serious consideration of purpose have only become more urgent. How can we get back to the raw power of the idea of purpose and jettison the ambiguity, complacency, and ritualization that have grown up around it?

What is Purpose?

Purpose is developed at the intersection of aspiration, external need, and action. A purpose is an *enduring* aspiration formed around a need in the world that a company is willing and able to act on, using either intrinsic strengths or capabilities it could develop. For example, the world's oldest company, Japanese construction firm Kongō Gumi, describes its purpose this way: "Kongō Gumi constructs shrines

---

1 Christopher A. Bartlett and Sumantra Ghoshal, "Beyond Strategy to Purpose," *Harvard Business Review*, November-December 1994. https://hbr.org/1994/11/beyond-strategy-to-purpose [accessed 9/5/2020].

https://doi.org/10.1515/9783110697834-006

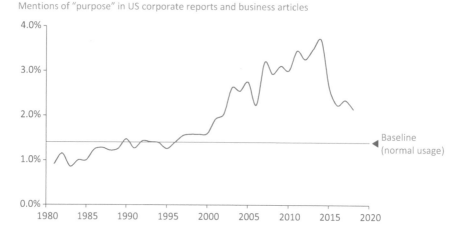

Mentions of "purpose" in US corporate reports and business articles

Figure 6.1: Popular Interest in the Idea of Business Purpose.

and temples that cultivate and bring calmness to your mind."[2] Although the company has probably articulated this purpose in different ways over time, and its offering and operations have evolved (the company was recently acquired), it has pursued the core social good of bringing calm to people's minds since its founding 1,440 years ago.

At the heart of the idea of purpose are a number of discomforting tensions (Figure 6.2). There is the tension between idealism and realism: on the one hand, you want to set forth an ideal that pushes your company to become something greater than it is currently, but on the other hand, you don't want videos and speeches articulating lofty aspirations that are grossly mismatched with your company's intention and capability to act. Reality without ideals takes you nowhere, but ideals without reality are equally fruitless – you end up either ignoring the ideal or pretending you are already living it.

Then there is the tension between imagination and existing needs. One can be guided by a dream – of what people's lives or society could be like – using it as the basis for articulating a new need. Or one can set out to meet a palpable existing need. Serving acknowledged needs is likely to be more realistic but also to provide less differentiation from others. Shaping new needs offers greater possibilities for uniqueness and profit but is likely to be less feasible.

---

2 Kongō Gumi was bought in 2006 by the Takamatsu Construction Group after 1428 years of independence; https://www.takamatsu-cg.co.jp/eng/about/group/takamatsu/kongogumi. html [accessed 9/5/2020].

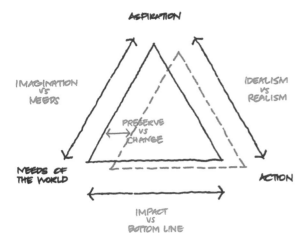

Figure 6.2: Tensions at the Heart of the Idea of Purpose.

There is also the tension between having a positive impact on society and maintaining financial viability. When addressing an ideal cannot generate a return, the purpose will not be sustainable. On the other hand, when the need is conceived as little more than providing a useful product, the purpose is hardly inspiring. The tension is between fulfilling a societal need and keeping the machine of the business running to fund the purpose on a sustainable basis.

Finally, there is the tension between consistency of purpose over time and adaptation to changing conditions. On the one hand, a commitment that can be broken and reframed too easily is not a principled basis for an enduring identity. On the other, aspirations, needs, and capabilities all change over time, indicated by the dotted triangle in Figure 6.2; it is natural that even if your purpose endures, how you understand and act on it evolves as you experiment and learn in a changing world.

A good purpose integrates and balances all of these tensions. It is a balance of idealism (setting a real aspiration) and realism (not ignoring brutal truths); it is an imaginative way to meet a genuine need; it suggests a path for making an impact while attracting and maintaining sufficient resources to do so; and it captures what is timeless while leaving room for evolution of thought and action.

Why do we Still Need Purpose?

Pursuing a purpose offers a number of benefits for an organization. A purpose can align the many parts of a company, defining the common aspiration that binds them together. It can explain how what a company does is significant and inspiring: how day-to-day work – building Japanese temple walls, making windshield wipers, monitoring social media content – contributes to a higher goal. It can create a basis for innovative thinking by highlighting the gap between an ideal and reality and hinting at new products and services that need to be invented in order to bridge that gap. And it can help build resilience in the face of business and social change, including changing personnel in the company. New waves of people inherit a guiding aspiration to make their own, to pursue in their own way in new circumstances.

There are several reasons why getting purpose right is a high priority today. One is the increased pressure on business leaders. In a 2018 survey of people in 28 countries, about 80% of people said they expect CEOs to be personally visible[3] in sharing the company's purpose, and around 75% want CEOs to discuss how their company benefits society.

Another is the political polarization of democracies and the increasing impact of political and social issues on business. Not every company will be pulled in front of regulators as Facebook and Twitter were, but one component of a sustainable relationship with customers, regulators, and other stakeholders is having an authentic answer to the question of what one's company adds to society.

Additionally, the growing complexity and scale of the corporation make it increasingly necessary to create an overarching narrative and set of beliefs that bind it together.

Finally, as is widely known, most employees are disengaged at work – 85%, according to a recent Gallup survey. For most people today, companies don't inspire the energy and commitment one gets from being part of a collective effort to accomplish a worthwhile purpose.

How to Rediscover the Benefits of Purpose

A purpose can easily become routinized and trivialized. After some initial excitement, the slogan becomes familiar and the thinking that led to it is forgotten. Even

---

3 "2018 Edelman Trust Barometer," *Edelman*, January 21, 2018. https://www.edelman.com/research/2018-edelman-trust-barometer [accessed 9/5/2020].

if we set out with a sincere intention to build something greater, it's easy to become so focused on the means that we think rarely, if ever, about the ends. We settle back into maintaining existing routines, making familiar products via well-defined processes. And we tend to avoid difficult questions and tensions raised by the serious pursuit of purpose.

So how can we recover the benefits of purpose and make it a useful and transformative concept? We need to face up to some difficult issues and imperatives.

- *Purpose must be discomforting:* When you set a purpose, you create a gap between aspiration and reality. A purpose should make you feel that what you are doing now is not enough. Both the insight about what to do and the motive to do it come from thinking about this gap: holding both the ideal and the reality in mind at once. Forgetting one or the other reduces discomfort but also removes the motivation for action.

  For example, Nestlé's purpose is "enhancing quality of life and contributing to a healthier future." To be effective, this has to be discomforting. The purpose should prompt Nestlé to ask, how can we contribute *more and better*? Answering this question should stimulate the imagination, leading to ideas for new products and services, M&A in new areas, and corporate statesmanship in issues concerning quality of life and health.

- *Creating a purpose is about clarifying a timeless idea:* It can be useful to dig back to the roots of a company: purpose should be linked to identity formed over time, and looking at earlier motivations and inspirations can help in finding the common thread. However, the easy way to make a purpose is just to give a pithy summary of what you happen to have been doing so far. The more discomforting but productive path is to drill down to a core, timeless good, which will form the heart of the purpose going forward, even if the way this good is articulated and pursued evolves over time.

  Meeting a need in the world involves bringing something good to people. A "good" is simply something valuable and could be described at many levels: good for people in general (bringing joy), a valuable product or service (office chairs, therapy), or a particular moment (when friends share stories). The best purposes latch on to a timeless good related to collective flourishing. For example, a retail bank might have spent its existence focusing on convenience and security, but we might see the underlying good as, say, bringing organization and wisdom around money into people's lives. Setting up this greater good as the aspiration creates the discomforting but necessary tension between the past and the present.

- *Purpose requires thinking through the key phenomena:* Whether a purpose is just a tagline or a serious aspiration depends on the depth of understanding behind it. If a company had the purpose "to bring joy to the world," for example, we should want to find out the substance of its thinking around joy. Why is joy valuable? When does it appear and for how long? What makes it authentic rather than superficial? And how has the company linked this understanding of joy to its current and future capabilities to create it?

Take BCG's purpose as another example: "to unlock the potential of those who advance the world." The timeless good here is unlocking people's potential. To pursue this seriously, we must ask how this happens and use this to define the evolution of our capabilities to make this happen more often or more effectively. This is rightly discomforting, but pursued rigorously it could lead to a new kind of inspiring organization.

- *Purpose requires honest communication:* Purpose is shared, so a lack of good communication can undermine it. The tempting path in communicating a purpose is to focus just on the upside. This is understandable: we want the launch event to be enjoyable, and so we look at the appealing side of the purpose, while forgetting any uncomfortable implications and the gritty, messy nature of the actual business.

  Focusing solely on the upside can end up having little effect, however: people see the purpose as a glossy, sentimentalized picture that has little to do with the actual nature of the work. A better option may be to tackle head-on the ideal-reality gap. It may be discomforting, but acknowledging the challenge that the purpose throws down, given where we are now, is the first step toward taking substantive action.

- *Purpose should lead you in unusual directions:* A purpose should prompt action in new directions rather than just summarizing and preserving the status quo. It should therefore shape your M&A and R&D strategies, your product portfolio, internal processes, and your corporate statesmanship activities.

  To continue our example, imagine that a bank set the purpose of cultivating wisdom and organization around money. It could act on this by developing tools to help with self-control, developing a new service to offer financial education to teenagers, or, more ambitiously, acquiring a counseling company to train a new kind of therapist-banker who would help people probe and reflect on their motivations around money. By so doing, the bank might become the leading voice for self-reflection around our individual and collective attitudes toward money. Letting purpose drive action can lead you in new and potentially fruitful directions.

Setting a purpose is an easy exercise when it doesn't involve discomfort or change. Instead, we should embrace the productive tensions of purpose, which will inspire action. The purpose of purpose is to change the current reality, not to justify it.

Martin Reeves, Simon Levin, Jack Fuller, and Fabien Hassan
Chapter 7
Your Change Needs a Strategy

Companies frequently need to change themselves, in more or less dramatic ways. If change is ambitious with respect to degree or timescale, we often call it "transformation." This is a difficult process that often does not work: our research shows that even with modest criteria, only about one-quarter of transformations succeed.[1]

The standard approach to organizational change is a linear project management mindset: define the target state of the organization, determine the logical sequence of action steps, then execute. In reality, though, there are many different kinds of change, each with its own requirements and risks. There are different types of transformations and different components of change within each. General advice on how to do transformation well risks ignoring this variety of potential change strategies. A better approach is to de-average transformation into its different components and ask, what does it take to succeed in each?

The Landscape of Possibility

One way of describing change comes from evolutionary biology. Change can be understood as movement across a "landscape of possibility," where each point on the landscape corresponds to a possible state of an organization. Higher organizational performance corresponds to greater "height" in the landscape. In pursuing organizational change, we might have a vision of a specific peak and set a course toward it, or we might be tracking upward along an unclear path.

In business, as in evolutionary biology, the topography of our landscape is also shifting. As the economy and competitive conditions change over time, new peaks may rise up (perhaps enabled by new technologies), or new clear paths might open (perhaps enabled by new practices).

1 Martin Reeves, Lars Fæste, Kevin Whitaker, and Fabien Hassan, "The Truth About Corporate Transformation: Empirical analysis reveals that conventional wisdom about big, risky change initiatives is often wrong." *MITSloan Management Review*, January 31, 2018. https://sloanreview.mit.edu/article/the-truth-about-corporate-transformation/ [accessed 9/5/2020].

https://doi.org/10.1515/9783110697834-007

Using this framework, we can investigate the various strategies for pursuing organizational change, the context in which each is appropriate, and the tactics required to succeed in each. In particular, we can consider these change strategies along two axes: the clarity we have about the ends (the target state for the organization), and the clarity we have about the means to get there (Figure 7.1).

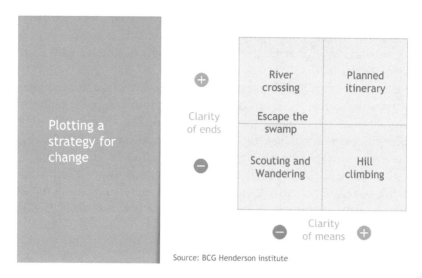

Source: BCG Henderson Institute

Figure 7.1: Plotting a Strategy for Change.

Change Strategies and Tactics

Each of the following strategies represents a different kind of journey across the landscape of possibility. We discuss different change strategies, when they should be applied, as well as the tactics required to succeed in each (Figure 7.2).

Change Strategy 1: Planned Itinerary

Perhaps the most familiar strategy of change is the "planned itinerary." The strategy is based on a clear idea of both the end and the means. Driven by a vision of a destination, we aim to follow a precisely planned path toward it.

This approach sounds ideal: it is predictable, readily comprehensible, and easily communicable to employees and investors. Indeed, we have an innate tendency to think in terms of planned itineraries. Psychological research suggests

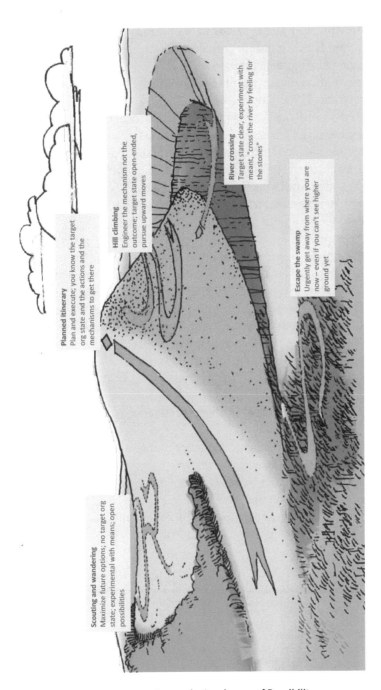

Planned itinerary
Plan and execute; you know the target org state and the actions and the mechanisms to get there

Hill climbing
Engineer the mechanism not the outcome; target state open-ended, pursue upward moves

River crossing
Target state clear, experiment with meant, "cross the river by feeling for the stones"

Escape the swamp
Urgently get away from where you are now – even if you can't see higher ground yet

Scouting and wandering
Maximize future options; no target org state; experimental with means; open possibilities

Figure 7.2: Different Journeys Across the Landscape of Possibility.

that our default interpretive frame is to look for a goal and a series of actions that lead to that end. Even if a clear goal or path does not exist, we may invent these components to rationalize our thought process.[2]

Yet the appeal of this strategy might tempt us to apply it even in situations where it is not warranted. We may believe that if we do A and B our organization will reach its predetermined destination, but in practice, the path turns out to be more complicated. In uncertain circumstances, the confidently crafted plan becomes detrimental. To illustrate, a health insurance company might aim to digitize all of its customer transactions. The CEO puts forward an itinerary with a timeline of actions and sensible intended outcomes, but the actual rollout of the new system causes unpredicted interdepartmental confusion and delays for customers.

We should be careful to apply this approach only when we are justifiably confident that the known means will achieve a predefined goal. For example, in 2016 Staples set out to reduce the costs of goods sold[3] by negotiating with its suppliers. The target was clear: save $250 million across its inventory. And the means were well-known and reliable: list all the currently sold products, request proposals from alternative suppliers, and negotiate with them to reduce costs. The expected savings could be estimated with reasonable accuracy, and the change process was carried through to meet this target.

What Tactics are Required to Succeed in "Planned Itinerary"?

The basic tools in this case are the familiar ones of change management:
- Describe the overall vision in a compelling way.
- Define the key success metrics that follow from this vision.
- Set milestones and create Gantt charts.
- Divide the work into stages and define clear accountabilities.
- Manage the process centrally from a program office.

2 Csibra, Gergely and Gergely, G. (2007) "Obsessed with goals": functions and mechanisms of teleological interpretation of actions in humans. ActaPsychologica 124 (1), pp. 60–78. ISSN 0001-6918. http://eprints.bbk.ac.uk/472/1/csibra1.pdf?origin%3Dpublication_detail [accessed 9/5/2020].
3 Phil Wahba, "How Staples Plans to Come Back After U.S. Kills Office Depot Merger," *Fortune*, May 10, 2016. https://fortune.com/2016/05/10/staples-office-depot-merger-2/ [accessed 9/5/2020].

The leader's mindset should be focused on efficiency – we can give full rein to our inbuilt tendency to consider action in goal-directed, hierarchical terms. We need a single-minded focus on the target state of the organization, and the required toughness to cut off anything that is not helping in pursuit of this end.

Internal communication can be largely one-way. The focus is on clarity: to define roles and align intentions, rather than maximizing openness to new initiatives and ideas from below. The information flow in the reverse direction centers on feedback on the attainment of targets and obstacles encountered. External communication is straightforward in this case – one can explain the proposed goal and actions to secure buy-in from stakeholders.

Change Strategy 2: River Crossing

In certain contexts, we are unable to gain clarity on the means of change. In this case, the appropriate change strategy is one we call "river crossing." The end state is clear, but we need an exploratory approach to the path, taking one step at a time while keeping an eye on our destination. To use the phrase coined by Deng Xiaoping to describe his reform effort, we need to "cross the river by feeling for the stones."

An example of this strategy in business is the transformation of Starbucks in 2008–2009. As the company he founded faced declining same-store sales and worsening financial performance, Howard Schultz reinstated himself as CEO to address the troubles. Schultz's sense of where the organization needed to be was strong. Starbucks needed to restore the emotional attachment and loyalty that customers used to have for the company, to "make each store the heart of the local neighborhood." But the means to get there were less clear; they would just "have to find a way."

Schultz's team pursued multiple efforts, but their main area of experimentation and discovery was social media. In 2008, this was still an unfamiliar area for most corporations, but Starbucks took an organic approach: as one senior executive said, they "didn't over-plan it." They started a Facebook page, posting community stories and bold political messages (e.g., petitioning congress to pass a budget agreement). On Twitter, they tried replying directly to complaints and suggestions, breaking with common practice at the time. The results were exceptional: Starbucks soon became the first company to reach 1 million

Facebook fans, rising to 27 million in 2010. The enhanced customer loyalty paid off with consecutive years of record annual revenues thereafter.[4]

When is this change strategy appropriate to apply? We can adopt it out of necessity, when we don't know the path to reach the target state of our organization; or if we have the time and resources, we can leave the means open-ended by choice, to allow directed exploration and discovery.

What Tactics are Required to Succeed in "River Crossing"?

The river crossing change strategy requires a distinctive toolkit, based on the fact that it combines goal-directedness and experimentation. A central program office is still helpful, but rather than planning all the efforts, its focus should be on assessing whether the various experiments are progressing the organization toward the goal – and amplifying those that are.

The organizational tools required in this strategy are:
- Pilots, with a focus on potential for scaling
- Systematic assessment of experiments
- Flexible resource reallocation toward the most promising ideas
- Culture that values experimentation and learning over prudence
- A case study team to identify and learn from other organizations that have taken similar journeys

The leadership mindset in this case must combine the equally important poles of openness to experiment and a focus on efficiency. An exploratory mind is required to dream up initiatives, but these experiments should not obscure the goal: the portfolio of bets must be managed and assessed through the lens of the overall target state. Leaders must constantly ask both expansive and focusing questions:
- Are we experimenting in the right directions, or are we missing a possible path?
- Which of these efforts might get us to where we want to go? Which paths are proving fruitless and how can we narrow down to focus on what is working?

---

4 Nancy F. Koehn, Kelly McNamara, Nora N. Khan and Elizabeth Legris, "Starbucks Coffee Company: Transformation and Renewal," *Harvard Business School, HBS Case Collection*, June 2014. https://www.hbs.edu/faculty/Pages/item.aspx?num=47471 [accessed 9/5/2020].

Communication may be trickier, because this approach requires us to admit our ignorance (Schultz talked about the difficulty of "having to artfully convey that he did not, in fact, have all the answers"). Yet the open-ended aspect of the task can also be used to spur people's creativity and participation.

Change Strategy 3: Hill Climbing

Unlike river crossing, where we start with a goal and try to figure out the means to get there, in "hill climbing" we start with the means. We engineer a particular mechanism, but we are open-minded about precisely how this will change the organization – either because we can't know, or because it is useful to leave this open-ended. We call this strategy hill climbing, because we are not aiming for a well-defined peak, but rather focusing on a series of good next steps that will lead us upward.

Such an approach is often applicable to an evolving technology. For example, the farm equipment company John Deere has been investing heavily in Internet of Things (IoT) technology.[5] They have begun by adding sensors to seed planters and harvesters that send data to programs, allowing farmers to monitor inputs, conditions, and outputs in a granular fashion. This of course opens the possibility for longitudinal analytics to improve efficiency over time, and also the potential for John Deere to integrate data from multiple farms to provide advice, as well as refine their own machinery.

In this case, the overall trend in the growing importance of IoT is clear, so anything that contributes to developing the IoT readiness is desirable. Ron Zink, the company's director of on-board applications, describes their open-ended approach: "[With products] that are doing well, you build from those and create a broader service around them." The value of these products, and the broader services the company will offer, are still being discovered. One cannot say precisely how this will shape John Deere, but it is clear that business model innovation using IoT technology is an "uphill" move. In fact, trying to tie the company to a tightly defined target state would be limiting; keeping the change open-ended allows the business to take advantages of unforeseen opportunities as they arise.

---

5 "John Deere turns to IoT to make smart farming a reality," *Internet of Business*. https://internetofbusiness.com/john-deere-turns-iot-smart-farming/ [accessed 9/5/2020].

What Tactics are Required to Succeed in "Hill Climbing"?

Hill climbing is not directed by an overall goal, so it involves a fundamentally different toolkit and mindset than planned itinerary or river crossing. Here the priority is on running experiments intended to drive some kind of positive change in the organization, but not one precisely defined in advance.

The most basic difference is that instead of asking, "Are we on track?" we ask, "What effect is this having?" Rather than developing criteria and metrics to determine if the overall target state has been achieved, we watch the organization as observers, to see what we can learn from how it is changing. Progress reports, in this strategy of change, should therefore not start with an assessment of progress against a plan and an updated timeline, but with exciting observations, which may spur us to think of new uphill moves.

Upward communication is crucial – leaders should want to hear from the developers and frontline teams about how things are going and what opportunities they uncover for creating value. Customer research is also central: as John Deere adds in IoT technology to its products, it might hear from farmers about innovative ways they are using the capabilities. With these feedback loops in place, the organization may change into something no one could have foreseen, realizing new forms of value that no one could have predicted.

Communication from leaders should focus on the excitement of unknown potential. Rather than being as clear as possible about what is intended and who is doing what – the familiar planned itinerary approach – leaders should focus on how they are staying flexible and excited about the unknown performance peaks the business might discover.

Change Strategy 4: Scouting and Wandering

There is a strategy for change, odd as it may seem, that is organized around neither a clear end state nor clear means. This change is not driven by immediate moves that seem obviously good, nor by any target state, but by curiosity, of a kind that will be useful in the long run. We can call it "scouting and wandering."

"Wandering" may sound illegitimate in business. This is partly because we are conditioned to drive toward clear outcomes. In R&D, however, we frequently see the value of a more open-ended approach. Google Labs was a forum for testing and tinkering with product ideas – wandering around the landscape of possible offerings. While much of its rambling exploration went nowhere, over its life, the Labs produced Gmail and other valuable products.

We can take a similar approach to business change: a company can invest in small experiments – in ways of working, technologies, HR policies, or any aspect of the business – with the aim of discovering directions for change for the business as a whole. Scouting and wandering is thus often a precursor strategy: if promising paths are discovered, it may be followed by a more goal-directed form of change.

To return to the metaphor of the landscape, the peaks and valleys are always shifting, as competitive conditions change and some business models lose their advantage, while new possibilities for peaks of performance open up. The scouting and wandering strategy can be adopted to hedge against the decline of the current model and to discover new upward paths, even if a company is doing well.

What Tactics are Required to Succeed in "Scouting and Wandering"?

Unlike previous strategies, scouting and wandering is not driven by a particular means or an end. Instead, firms must adopt tactics to be productively curious at a corporate level. One such mechanism is to set up in-house venture capital funds. Such funds can be manifestations of corporate curiosity about possible business models. With limited budgets, these funds do not aim to transform the whole organization, but they have dedicated market-watching teams and quick decision processes to enable fast action if they see an interesting startup. Today, 50% of all equity financing in fintech is backed by at least one incumbent. The banks are not immediately overhauling their core business; they are securing their position in case large-scale fintech disruption materializes and current business models become obsolete.

Wandering is not preplanned, but there are some ways to wander effectively. We can draw a lesson here from foraging patterns in nature. An effective pattern is to explore mostly nearby options, with an occasional leap into some faraway territory – called a "Lévy flight."[6] The local moves ensure that nearby, accessible opportunities are scouted, while the more radical moves ensure that broader territory is also searched. In the realm of organizational change, therefore, experiments should involve a mix of tinkering and radical moves.

---

6 Reynolds A. M. "Fitness-maximizing foragers can use information about patch quality to decide how to search for and within patches: optimal Levy walk searching patterns from optimal foraging theory." *J R Soc Interface*. 2012, 9(72): 1568–1575.

The leadership mindset for this strategy is similar to the one used when playing. One aspect of this is the ability to improvise, to try out some low-cost, low-regret action simply to see what might happen and to foster unexpected learning. Another aspect is imagination: the capacity to combine elements of what is known to explore the unknown. Also, in play, one is able to suspend goals, to open the way for unconstrained wandering. The mindset is thus similar to the observational, open-minded attitude in hill climbing, with the difference that one is not focused on pursuing a specific mechanism, but rather a varied set of efforts heading in different directions. Leaders should give permission to their teams to improvise – to run their own set of interesting experiments exploring different hunches and leads about ways the business might one day work.

Change Strategy 5: Escape the Swamp

The fifth kind of change strategy is one driven by the need to move away from where you are now. Like scouting and wandering, this is not driven by a particular means, and the only clear aspect of the goal is that it must involve substantial and urgent change. We can call this "escape the swamp." It applies in pressured situations such as the early stages of a turnaround, where there is limited time or resources to identify specific ends or means, but we are nevertheless driven to change.

The decline of Blockbuster[7] is an example of when this strategy would be necessary. Due to the rapidly shifting landscape of the industry, Blockbuster found itself in a "swamp," when a few years before it had been on a peak. It was unclear exactly how Blockbuster should respond to the success of Netflix; there was arguably no obvious organizational state that the company should aim to transform into, nor any clear and powerful initial moves to make. The only thing that was clear – unfortunately – was that it needed to move away from where it was. This kind of strategy comes from desperation: it makes sense to try radical moves, because only something radical *might* get you out of the swamplands.

---

7 Larry Downes and Paul Nunes, "Blockbuster Becomes a Casualty of Big Bang Disruption," *Harvard Business Review*, November 7, 2013. https://hbr.org/2013/11/blockbuster-becomes-a-casualty-of-big-bang-disruption [accessed 9/5/2020].

What Tactics are required to Succeed in "Escape the Swamp"?

The essential organizational tools in this strategy are concerned with fast action and orchestrating dramatic levels of change. As the driver of the change is the need to escape the current situation under time pressure, it makes sense for decision making to be centralized. This is because many people will be invested in the current state, but there is often not enough time to persuade people widely of the need for a drastic move. Instead, the change should be driven by a core group that *does* see the urgency.

The decision making in this strategy is about trading off between two risks: the risk of wasting time (and sinking further into the swamp) and the risk of making a disastrous move (inadvertently jumping into something worse). Leaders should reduce the risks of error by gathering information about the situation and possible options, but often both of these risks will be high and there is an element of luck in success here.

Leaders pursuing this strategy must be skilled at communicating urgency to the relevant stakeholders, while also maintaining resolve and not spreading panic. It thus requires a judicious mix of honesty (enough to create necessary alarm) and diplomacy (to hide one's true feelings, when necessary, to avoid spreading unproductive panic). It also requires courage, because a small tinkering move will generally not be enough to get out of the situation.

Competition and Cooperation in Change

We might assume that in business change we are dealing with an optimization problem: given what we know of our ends and means, what's the best way to reengineer or intervene in our company? But this approach misses a key input, the "game theory" element of business change: how your change strategy is affected by what other players are doing. We know that attempts to optimize the best route, when others are doing exactly the same, can make things worse for everyone: it has been shown that route-finding apps for cars, when widely adopted, can make overall traffic worse.[8]

---

8 Alexandre Bayen, "The Impact of Routing Apps on Traffic," *Tencent WE Summit, YouTube*, November 16, 2017. https://www.youtube.com/watch?v=nx-QTOBIPZw [accessed 9/5/2020].

To understand the social aspect of change, we can turn again to evolutionary theory.[9] If we picture companies as foragers, we can imagine groups of them moving across the landscape of possibility, looking for high-performing spots. If there is a large territory where it is easy to find high-performing positions, then it makes sense to pay less attention to what others are doing and focus instead on moving there as fast as possible. John Deere's efforts around IoT fall into this category. At this time, the technology is in early stages and there are many opportunities opening up. Businesses should focus on experimenting and implementing the technology internally, rather than defining change strategy in relation to other players.

On the other hand, areas of the landscape become crowded over time, and we are then faced with the question of whether to collaborate or compete. That is, to work with others, incorporating them and what they can offer into the business change strategy; or to compete, defining the change strategy against others and what they might do, to set up a defensible territory. In nature, this choice depends on the exploitation potential of a particular location. If a business can extract a large amount of value from a position, now and into the future, it should design its change strategy to exclude others and entrench itself. For example, if Standard Oil had undergone a transformation around 1900, the strategy would be informed not only by what the company needed to run effectively but also how to undercut or lock out competitors. It had found a position with huge exploitation potential, and all that was needed was to defend its spot and get on with exploiting.

In other situations, though, it may be more beneficial to cooperate. Cooperation tends to occur when value is hard to exploit. We can see this in the current efforts of multiple companies to exploit the potential of driverless cars,[10] ranging from Samsung to Volkswagen to Baidu. The prize is large but it is hard to reach it, requiring cooperation across distant sectors. Change strategies for each of these players should revolve around making the best use of partnerships – a consideration that depends on what potential partners are thinking, and how they are changing, too.

9 Christopher T Monk, Matthieu Barbier, Pawel Romanczuk, James R Watson, Josep Alós, Shinnosuke Nakayama, Daniel I Rubenstein, Simon A Levin, Robert Arlinghaus, "How ecology shapes exploitation: a framework to predict the behavioural response of human and animal foragers along exploration-exploitation trade-offs," *Ecol Lett*. 2018 Jun; 21(6):779–793. doi: 10.1111/ele.12949. Epub 2018 Apr 2. https://pubmed.ncbi.nlm.nih.gov/29611278/ [accessed 9/5/2020].
10 Christina Mercer and Tom Macaulay, "Companies working on driverless cars: Which companies are working on driverless cars? The companies developing autonomous vehicles, from traditional carmakers such as BMW, Mercedes-Benz and Toyota to tech giants including Apple, Baidu and Waymo," *Tech Advisor*, June 27, 2019. https://www.techadvisor.co.uk/fea ture/small-business/-companies-working-on-driverless-cars-3788696/ [accessed 9/5/2020].

Cooperation is also beneficial when resources are patchy, when it is hard to identify where the good opportunities will be. One example in business is app development: Apple and Facebook saw the potential in apps but couldn't identify in advance what the successful apps would be. So they cooperated, sharing profits with smaller developers to explore the space. The current prevalence of ecosystems in business is a testament to these effects.

Sometimes, then, we can afford to ignore others, but in crowded territory our change strategy should be informed by whether we are aiming to secure our position or cooperate – or as is often the case, some combination of these, as different aspects of a complex change effort.

Sequencing Change

Change can be a comparatively simple process that requires just one of our five approaches. Or it may be complex, requiring multiple change strategies to be combined in parallel or in series. One corporate transformation might involve multiple change strategies. A company might begin with a strategy of escape the swamp and, after a few successful dramatic moves to head off disaster, move into a planned itinerary strategy to drive cost savings, and then a river crossing strategy for a long-term experimental effort to evolve the company's core business model.

Combining strategies is especially important in scenarios that involve hill climbing. Pursued alone, this strategy may lead to getting stuck on local peaks, if you're only guided by making immediate good moves upward. Sometimes you need to come down off a small hill to find a larger one. It often makes sense to sequence hill climbing with scouting and wandering. In the study of optimizing complex systems, this is called "simulated annealing" – interspersing random exploration to ensure you don't get stuck.[11]

Even if such change efforts are connected in a sequence, each should be governed according to its own special dynamics, as we have seen. Each requires a distinct set of organizational tools and approaches, a unique leadership mindset, and a tailored approach to communication. Leaders and organizations need to master the art of diagnosing situations and combining change strategies.

---

11 Kirkpatrick, Scott, C. Daniel Gelatt, and Mario P. Vecchi. "Optimization by simulated annealing." *science* 220.4598 (1983): 671–680. https://science.sciencemag.org/content/220/4598/671 [accessed 9/5/2020].

Crucially, they also must develop capabilities to drive multiple kinds of change, often at the same time across different parts of the business. We can call this capacity "change ambidexterity."

Developing the right sequence of change strategies begins with diagnosis. There are seven diagnostic questions that leaders should ask at the outset:

1. What is the urgency to move away from the current situation?
2. How clear is the end state?
3. How clear are the means to get there?
4. Should we go it alone, collaborate, or compete toward our goal?
5. What stages of change do we need to move through?
6. What is the optimal strategy for each, and what does this imply at the level of tactics?
7. Do we have the required capabilities, and if not, how will we build them?

When it comes to transformation, it is tempting to seek simplicity. We generally adopt a single approach to change, which is more often than not a planned itinerary. But changing a complex system while also keeping it running is never so simple. A better approach is to acknowledge the complexity, the risks, and the unknowns, and to deploy tailored change strategies suited to the different parts of the journey.

Part II: **Managing the Change Strategy**

Peter Tollman, Perry Keenan, Stéphanie Mingardon,
Diana Dosik, Shaheer Rizvi, and Stephanie Hurder

Chapter 8
Getting Smart About Change Management

The business world, like the geopolitical world, has entered a new age of uncertainty. Turbulence is affecting more and more industries – more frequently and more severely. One-time market leaders and corporate giants fall rapidly from grace, having failed to modernize or having lost out to nimble competitors. BlackBerry and Blockbuster are among the high-profile casualties. In fact, companies are expiring sooner than ever before: data suggests that one-third of all public companies will disappear within the next five years.[1]

Companies are facing a new reality, one of economic unpredictability, disruptive technology, globalization, and unprecedented fierce competition. In such an environment, traditional sources of advantage like scale and proprietary assets are no longer so valuable or sustainable. The priority imperative for many businesses is to adapt to the changing conditions in order to boost performance – or even to survive.[2] To paraphrase Darwin, it's not the strongest of the species that survives, but the most adaptable.

One industry that has been a huge beneficiary of all this turbulence is the change management industry. Companies in all sectors eagerly seek its services, on the premise that a tailor-made change program will improve the trajectory of their business. Unfortunately, change programs have a remarkably modest record of success. The traditional approach to change management is itself in need of change.

Over the past few years, the change management industry has been logging an average annual growth rate of 5%. Companies around the world now spend close to a whopping $10 billion a year on change management consultancy.[3] Publications and reports on the subject have proliferated. It has become a major

1 Martin Reeves and Lisanne Pueschel, "Die Another Day: What Leaders Can Do About the Shrinking Life Expectancy of Corporations," BCG Perspectives, July 2015. https://www.bcg.com/publications/2015/strategy-die-another-day-what-leaders-can-do-about-the-shrinking-life-expectancy-of-corporations [accessed 9/5/2020].
2 Martin Reeves and Michael S. Deimler, "New Bases of Competitive Advantage: The Adaptive Imperative," BCG Perspectives, October 2009. https://www.bcg.com/publications/2009/business-unit-strategy-new-bases-of-competitive-advantage [accessed 9/5/2020].
3 ALM Intelligence, "Competitive Landscape Analysis: Change Management Consulting," 2016.

https://doi.org/10.1515/9783110697834-008

discipline at many business schools. Organizations are conscientiously incorporating it into their operating models: in the decade between 2003 and 2013, according to a recent survey, the proportion of respondents adopting a "structured approach" to change management rose from 32% to 80%.[4]

Yet despite all the investment, the industry has not lived up to expectations. The evidence, including self-reported CEO data, indicates that 50% of change programs fail to achieve their objectives; the failure rate rises to 75% for more complex and ambitious programs. These rates have remained much the same for the past few decades. The failures are costly, translating into billions of dollars of lost potential value, not to mention the impact on senior executive turnover, most notably among CEOs.

Most Sectors are Experiencing Volatility Unmatched in Decades

To put this disappointing performance in perspective, consider how other industries have fared in recent history when tackling complex challenges of their own. Never mind computing, always the outlier, with its trillionfold increase in performance over the past 60 years.[5] Just think how the cost of airline tickets – or solar power, or oil extraction – has fallen in the past couple of decades. Even biopharmaceuticals, an industry with a remarkably complex set of challenges, has registered significant advances in treating various cancers, coronary artery disease, HIV/AIDS, and hepatitis C. In a broad cross-industry comparison, change management remains near the bottom of the performance table. It has not lived up to its promise. Indeed, by most metrics, it has failed.

The Four Fatal Errors of Change Programs

No matter what specific changes a change program is intended to bring about – a new operating model, a superior cost position, new sources of competitive

---

4 Prosci Change Management Webinar, "2014 Benchmarking Report: Top Contributors to Success," 2014.
5 Experts Exchange, "Processing Power Compared." https://singularityhub.com/2015/05/25/infographic-trillion-fold-rise-in-computing-puts-a-1985-supercomputer-on-our-wrists/ [accessed 9/5/2020].

advantage – the fundamental objectives are always the same: to improve performance, substantially and sustainably, and to establish an organization agile enough to adapt to future disruptions. Those aims necessarily involve a sustained change in employees' behavior and for that to occur, it must be in the individual interests of employees to change their behavior – or at least in their individual interests as they perceive them to be. After all, people don't willingly and proactively behave in ways that seem detrimental to their perceived interests. If employees are to commit to the change program and support it throughout, there has to be something in it for them as individuals.

The Smart and Simple Approach to Changing Performance

Company performance is determined by, or even tantamount to, the behavior of the company's workforce. *Behavior* can be defined simply as "what people do": the decisions they make, the actions they take, the interactions they engage in. What happens in a company – from its innovations to its customer service to its key processes and capabilities – is clearly a function of what people do.

Broadly, people pursue a rational strategy when it comes to behavior: they choose to behave in ways that are in their own perceived best interests. In other words, people adopt rational, "individually winning" behaviors. That is the foundation of *Smart Simplicity*. Which behaviors are rational is determined by an individual's current *context*; that is, the combination of rewarding or unrewarding factors that influence his or her actions, decisions, and interactions. (For most employees, a favorable context is one that provides job security and allows them to flourish in their careers. For employees nearing retirement, a favorable context might be one featuring a generous severance package; for younger employees, the ideal context might include flextime, or a prominent public role, or exciting travel opportunities.)

Viewed through the lens of Smart Simplicity, a company is a system of rational strategies pursued by individual employees. Fortunately, most of these strategies tend to be widely shared among the workforce. It's by understanding and shaping those strategies that executives can effect change. And the way to get individuals to change their strategies and hence their behavior sustainably – and consequently to boost company performance – is to change their contexts so that the behaviors conducive to the change program are also in the individuals' best interests.

In any change program, there will inevitably be losers as well as winners among the staff. One painful prospect is that some of them might have to be laid off, and others might have to take on roles that they did not originally want. However, all employees will still behave in their own perceived best interests, given the options available to them. So the challenge is to adjust the context in such a way that their best interests are served by cooperating as fully as possible with the program rather than resisting or undermining it.[6]

Unfortunately, only a minority of change programs will change employees' contexts sufficiently to produce the new behaviors that the program requires. Accordingly, many change efforts fail. Numerous factors can contribute to this failure, of course, but it's worth looking at four particular errors that companies tend to make repeatedly – *the four fatal errors*, so called because they fatally undermine change efforts and frequently the credibility of the people leading them. Like most of the best fatal errors, they seemed like excellent ideas at the time and remain extremely appealing, so companies keep repeating them – and keep getting the same results. Our formulation of the four errors is distilled from more than 50 years' collective observation of companies in all major industries around the world. For obvious reasons, the case studies cited below have been anonymized and hybridized.

Fatal Error 1: Neglecting Employees' Individual Interests

Consider the case of a global industrial goods company that wanted to improve its sales forecasting. Sales forecasting serves many purposes, and these can sometimes conflict with one another. For example, forecasting is used for setting expectations, both internally for budget purposes and externally for earnings guidance; but it's also used for determining manufacturing volumes and inventory-carrying levels. In making estimates, the company's sales-forecasting team proved consistently conservative, and each year the sales team ended up selling substantially more than was forecast. Stockouts would sometimes occur, therefore, and the manufacturing team was held responsible. So the manufacturing team ceased trusting the sales forecasts and started to add an unofficial, roughly calculated buffer to its production quotas. As it happens, the manufacturing team was not held responsible for excess inventory and

---

6 For a fuller discussion of this "rational strategy" approach to workplace behavior and hence to corporate performance, see *Six Simple Rules: How to Manage Complexity without Getting Complicated*, by Yves Morieux and Peter Tollman, Harvard Business Review Press, 2014.

therefore consistently erred on the side of overestimating the required inventory. In consequence, the company's annual inventory-carrying costs were $120 million higher than necessary.

The company duly set about changing its approach to forecasting in order to make it more reliable and more relevant for everyone involved. Senior leadership, including the CEO and COO, presented a compelling case for change and tailored messages for each of the three teams – forecasting, sales, and manufacturing. The forecasting team would have to review and update its techniques in order to improve the accuracy of its forecasts; the sales team would have to make contingency plans in the event of stockouts; and the manufacturing team would have to stop buffering and produce only as much as the forecast indicated. Such adjustments would be difficult, but they would materially reduce inventory costs and help the company meet critical profit goals. The response from the workforce appeared to be enthusiastic, and the program launched in a very positive spirit. All to no avail.

The trouble was that the designers of the change program had failed to consider people's individual interests. It's not enough to present a compelling case for change. Change practitioners might invoke the fashionable phrase "burning platform" to convey the sense of crisis; they might explain how the specified changes are in the company's interests and the collective interests of all employees; they might segment their audience carefully into different stakeholder groups and customize their appeals to each of them. Quite possibly, all employees will be convinced that the change program is in the collective interest, but many of them will still obstruct the program, perhaps unwittingly, by failing to adjust their behavior as required. (Arguably, this familiar outcome has been an important force in shaping, or misshaping, the change management industry: many supposed experts have mistakenly characterized the obstructionists – especially those in middle management – as behaving emotionally or illogically, and have continued to refine their remedies for that imaginary malaise!)

In what way were individual interests opposed to the collective interest in this case? Why did conservative forecasting remain the rational choice for the forecasters? The underlying issue, which the leadership had overlooked, was that the forecasting team resided within the commercial division, which was compensated on the basis of sales performance relative to budgeted targets. It was in the forecasters' interest, therefore, to set conservative targets that they could then substantially exceed: in that way, they and their commercial-division coworkers would receive handsome bonuses. An accurate forecast, in contrast, would threaten and thereby incense the senior sales managers – the very people who could most affect a forecaster's salary or promotion prospects come the annual review.

The manufacturing team likewise had a perverse incentive: to overestimate upcoming sales and thereby reduce the risk of stockouts and the associated blame. The manufacturing team, however, had no power over the forecasting team and no way of encouraging it to provide higher forecasts. To avoid underproducing, the manufacturing team had no choice but to persist with the buffer. And because the team was not penalized for excess inventory, it tended to overproduce by a considerable margin. That is how the excess-inventory crisis was born.

As this case study demonstrates, the collective interest is all very well, but for individuals to change their behavior, it must be in their individual interests to do so. Inevitably, there will be some costs to employees in any change program, but the behaviors required for change can still be in their individual interests if there are benefits that, on balance, make it rational to get with the program. It's up to leadership to understand these cost-benefit analyses and tip the scales as needed to make active support of the collective change an individually winning strategy.

What happened at the industrial goods company when the program was launched? Nothing much, and that was the problem. The on-the-ground reality of the forecasters – their individual contexts – remained unchanged, so they had no real incentive to change their ways. They might have paid lip service to the rallying cries, and perhaps they even believed that they should and would comply with the change program by making more refined and less aggressive forecasts – but it was not in their individual interests to do so.

Despite the declared enthusiasm for a new style of forecasting, then, the forecasts remained conservative in practice and the manufacturing team continued to ignore them and overcompensate. The change effort was judged a failure, and its leader – a former rising star within the company – ended up leaving the firm.

Fatal Error 2: Underengaging the Extended Leadership Team

In advance of the launch of a major change program, it's crucial to get the extended leadership team seriously engaged. (In a large organization, this team consists of the top 150 executives or so.) Unfortunately, a great many companies delay such an engagement effort until well after the launch, and many never get around to it at all.

Take the case of a large bank that had attempted several change programs over five years without achieving any truly beneficial changes. Its most recent program was aimed at reducing risk-taking on the part of its loan officers. By selling financial products to high-risk borrowers, those loan officers had created serious problems in the past, and the company's loan portfolio was still worryingly exposed. The executive committee was eager to direct the loan officers' behavior toward greater prudence. A program management office (PMO) was promptly established, and, in concert with the executive committee, it duly devised and activated a change program.[7] The program sought to refocus front-line loan officers by pressing the standard levers – most notably, revising the incentive structure to encourage a long-term safety-first approach rather than a quick-profit approach.

Members of the extended leadership team, however, were generally left on the sidelines. They had little input into the program's design or early implementation. Instead of feeling like owners of the change, they felt underconsulted, underutilized, and underinformed – and, consequently, disrespected. Their direct reports sensed and therefore shared their lack of enthusiasm. For the workforce, accordingly, the PMO team had little credibility, and one year after launch the risk-reduction program remained largely unimplemented. Not surprisingly, the risk profile of borrowers showed no discernible difference from that of the previous year. When called to account by the board, the PMO ascribed the failure to "blockage from the extended leadership team" – referring to the leadership team's failure to amplify and support the PMO's reform agenda. Meanwhile, the riskier borrowers began defaulting in large numbers. The change program had proved to be little more than an expensive vanity exercise.

What the executive committee failed to realize is that engagement of the extended leadership team is pivotal in translating a change program's goals into actual workforce behaviors. No matter how inspiring the speeches from senior leaders may be, employees tend to listen to their direct manager more than to a C-suite executive. Proximity trumps seniority. They are aware that the direct manager has more influence over their professional fate – job security, status, salary increases, promotion prospects; and the direct manager, if properly engaged and equipped, is much better positioned to answer the crucial question, "What does the change mean for me, my team, and our customers?"

To align the rank and file with the change program, you need to get a critical mass of extended leadership team members on board – 70% or more, in our experience. Unless they have a personal stake in the change program, they will

---

7 The program management office – sometimes known by other names, such as the transformation office, in the context of change programs – is responsible for the day-to-day supervision and tracking of the change effort.

likely have little commitment to it and little incentive to rally the rest of the workforce. This personal stake can be generated in several ways. Give the extended leadership team members a voice earlier on in the program, for example, and they will feel a greater sense of ownership and will contribute more readily. In fact, their involvement should begin as early as the design stage – after all, they know the workforce and the situation on the ground better than the PMO or the senior sponsors do. Giving them the opportunity for meaningful input will make them feel included in the program and enthusiastic about it, and will also help keep the program free of design flaws.

Fatal Error 3: Failing to Sufficiently Empower the PMO

An oil and gas company had been conducting refinery enhancements and other focused engineering projects, all supported by a technically proficient PMO. The company was now embarking on a more ambitious, enterprise-wide transformation aimed at greatly boosting uptime at the refineries and improving efficiencies between upstream and downstream operations – a program that was meant to generate more than $700 million in annual savings. Senior management assumed that the PMO, with its existing setup and staffing, could handle the transformation and so put it in charge. Given the PMO's impressive record, there seemed to be no reason to change its structure or composition.

A few months after launch, the simpler initiatives were progressing well. But the more complex initiatives, where the bulk of the value lay, had stalled. The change program as a whole was not delivering according to expectations, and senior management ordered a fundamental review.

The review attributed the setback largely to two broad issues: first, a failure to identify, flag, and address critical delivery risks for the more complex initiatives; and, second, an inability to confirm that all the crucial and interdependent factors were in place. The reason for those shortcomings, in turn, was that the PMO lacked adequate power. Power, in this context, is influence over things that are important to others. Having such influence allows one to affect outcomes related to their interests and thereby encourage them to modify their behavior. Power can derive from an obvious source, such as a reporting relationship, input into a performance review, or control over budgets. It can also derive from a subtler source, such as access to specialized information, a particular expertise, or the backing of a senior leader.

The PMO was unable to order a thorough risk assessment prior to launch, raise concerns with senior management and arrange a course correction, or compel initiative leaders to participate. When the PMO asked those leaders to issue regular reports on the status of key risks, most of them simply filled out the PMO's template without describing the risks sufficiently, without specifying changes in the risks' drivers or magnitude, and without discussing any need for support. Some of the initiative leaders did not even bother to fill out the template, despite multiple reminders from the PMO. All in all, the PMO was thwarted in one of its crucial roles – that of accurately distilling and communicating the risks involved, and thereby giving senior management the opportunity to mitigate them.

This type of failure is alarmingly common. A PMO should be a steward of value for a change program. To play that role effectively and support senior leadership properly, a PMO needs adequate power. And to gain that power, it needs sufficient visibility into the various units and the means to influence behavior in them, especially to increase cooperation across the enterprise. A PMO will also benefit if it has prominent rising stars or seasoned leaders on its staff: the presence of rising stars signals to the organization that the PMO is to be taken seriously, and the presence of seasoned leaders indicates the PMO's deep knowledge of and interest in the long-term performance of the organization. Absent such signals of power, initiative leaders will perceive the PMO as marginal rather than powerful, and it will have limited ability to shape people's behavior in line with the objectives of the program.

Fatal Error 4: Allocating "Set-and-Forget" Targets

A company may be keen to empower its initiative leaders, to entrust them with considerable autonomy over budgets and resource allocation. But this well-intentioned policy can break down when it comes to more complex change initiatives, especially those involving shifts in strategy or changes to an organization's operating model.

The case of a major credit card company illustrates the perils. Under a newly appointed CEO, the company was embarking on an ambitious transformation program centered on shifting to a lower-cost operating model. The program involved an array of initiatives, including a cost reduction target for each department. The organization had historically followed a distinctly "federated" model, in which departments were led by strong managers who all favored the same traditional procedure – being assigned a target and then being left alone to get on with reaching it. The new CEO, in furtherance of the transformation program and in keeping with her own more rigorous approach, attempted to introduce various organizational reforms: joint executive-level redesign of the governance model, C-level visibility into the progress of the program, an increase in cross-functional cooperation, and a consistent and systematic tracking scheme based on key milestones. The initiative leaders regarded all of this as an encroachment on their turf and a lack of trust in their ability to execute. They resisted. The CEO changed tack, not wishing to undermine them early on, and for the next three years simply announced the annual targets and let the departments take responsibility for them. The hope was that assigning the targets, and then standing back, would be enough.

Such a policy may work for simple initiatives, but for more complex initiatives it's almost always inadequate. Simply setting annual department-level targets will generate behaviors that are short-term and incremental without challenging the business model or striving for sustainably higher productivity. Complex change programs demand a more sophisticated model – a model that includes forward-looking indicators, allows for course corrections, encourages creative and cooperative solutions, including cross-department solutions, and keeps senior management appropriately involved.

The hands-off, set-and-forget model for allocating targets has three major shortcomings. First, if senior management neglects to inspire ambitions, to monitor progress and make proper course corrections, and to show sufficient engagement, then the initiative leaders will have little reason to go the extra mile. Presented with an annual target, they will likely focus on measures that aim simply to meet it – typically, shortsighted cost-cutting measures such as restricting travel or delaying recruitment. After all, such measures are far easier to implement, and far less threatening to the delivery of day-to-day business results, than broad long-term measures such as seeking sustainable savings through increased productivity. Taking the simpler path is the rational choice when you have a very serious day job and understandably want to minimize disruption. Unfortunately, the short-term measures don't change productivity fundamentally or sustainably. Sooner or later they are discontinued, and when that happens, the benefits evaporate.

Second, the initiative leaders will likely seek solutions specific to their own departments rather than pursue opportunities that might contribute to collective, cross-department success. In fact, those promising opportunities, potentially conferring a competitive advantage, often remain undiscovered since individual departments left to their own devices have no particular incentive to look beyond their silos. They might even have a disincentive to do so, because they may rightly worry that they wouldn't get their fair share of credit for the results or that it would be a futile mission and damaging to their prospects.

Finally, the hands-off model militates against lead-indicator metrics, timely interventions, and course correction. If senior leaders have little visibility into a departmental initiative, they cannot easily realize that things are going off track – through the pursuit of unsustainable, short-term measures – until it's too late to do anything about it.

So how did the credit card company fare? In the first year, almost all the departments met their targets. In the second year, most missed them. By the end of the third year, overall costs had returned to their original unsatisfactory level. So much for the transformation! Disappointed and exasperated, the CEO commissioned a detailed review to try to establish how the program had gone wrong. The review found that the program – just like several previous change programs – had emphasized quick-win streamlining rather than sustainable cost savings and that it had neglected to pursue, or even identify, attractive cross-department opportunities. The CEO should have stayed the course in the early days. When the initiative leaders resisted, she should have persevered in backing the program's original design, and, leveraging her executive team, she should have sought a sustained productivity boost by insisting on the rigorous tracking and management of initiatives.

The Root Cause: Failure to make the Change Rational for Individual Employees

The four fatal errors share one particularly salient feature. In all four case studies, the change program failed to get people truly on board – to get them to adopt behaviors that were aligned with the success of the program.

No matter what a change program aims to do – boost productivity, realize synergies from a postmerger integration, or implement an innovative business model – it must first and foremost secure the buy-in of the workforce. For that to happen, all employees need to see that supporting the program is feasible and is in their individual interests. Each of the four fatal errors, in its own way, obstructs that crucial buy-in, so the requisite behavioral changes do not take place, and the change program falters.

How should a company go about securing the support of employees for a change program and getting them to adjust their behavior in its service? Our approach is *Smart Simplicity*, a framework for understanding – and enhancing – modern organizations.[8]

---

8 For a full account, see Yves Morieux and Peter Tollman, *Six Simple Rules: How to Manage Complexity without Getting Complicated*, Harvard Business Review Press, 2014.

A Glimpse of Smart Simplicity

Smart Simplicity provides a new lens for viewing organization issues, one that is more effective than that of traditional management approaches and is particularly powerful for organizations intent on change. Its key premise is that corporate performance is based on employees' individual behavior (decisions, activities, interactions) and that employees choose behavior that is in their individual best interests, given their current contexts.

For a change program to succeed, then, the imperative is to change employees' contexts in such a way that the employees' perceived individual interests become aligned with the interests of the company as a whole, and that it makes sense for the employees to cooperate as a team in the service of those interests.

Desired behaviors can be elicited first by giving employees the *ability* to act in the organization's best interests – specifically, by giving them appropriate resources, removing constraints, and creating transparency about what they and others do; and second, by increasing employees' *desire* to act in the organization's best interests – in other words, motivating them – specifically, by linking consequences tightly to action, requiring reciprocity and eliminating dysfunctional self-sufficiency, and rewarding *cooperation*. (Cooperation, in this sense, involves taking actions to improve the performance of a colleague or the organization as a whole, even if inconvenient to oneself.)

Smart Simplicity recognizes that an organization is a system of the individual rational behaviors of the people who constitute it, so the way to change the performance of the organization is to make new behaviors rational.

Another helpful resource in this regard is the *Change Delta*, a framework – drawing on decades of change management experience across the globe – that company leaders can use to manage major organizational change. Its value lies in managing a *program* of change rather than an individual project or initiative.[9] Effective program management is concerned with fine-tuning the program's overall governance, empowering leadership at all levels, engaging the

---

9 Program management is the art of structuring and setting up for success an overall program of initiatives across the organization. Any large-scale change program will consist of many projects or initiatives, which may be heavily interdependent. Each project will have its own leader, one or more objectives, and a set of milestones and risks, and is well served by a variety of familiar project management tools. These tools are also sometimes applied to a *program* of change – with little success, because they are too refined for the purpose and fail to provide a clear view of the program's progress.

full organization, and providing visibility into the progress of the activities involved. It sets the project up for success.

The Change Delta converts the principles of Smart Simplicity into practice. It encourages the desired behaviors by making them rational. It ensures that individual employees are not only aligned with the objectives and norms of the change program, but also have reasons to actively engage with it so that they make the right decisions and execute them efficiently. The Change Delta's four components, or aspects, are strongly interdependent and jointly optimize the program's structure and implementation (Figure 8.1). Here is a brief account of the four components.[10]

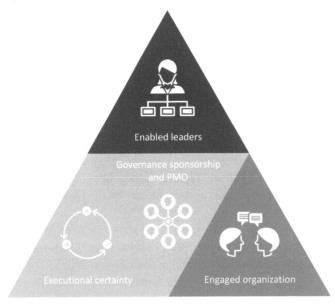

Note: PMO = Program management office
Source: BCG analysis

Figure 8.1: The Change Delta Is a Comprehensive Approach to Delivering Transformational Change.

---

10 A more detailed discussion can be found in "Changing Change Management: A Blueprint That Takes Hold," *BCG report*, December, 2012.

Governance: Sponsorship and PMO

The formal oversight of the change program – the governance – is typically the responsibility of two entities: the sponsor, or set of sponsors, and the PMO.

In the case of a company-wide change, the sponsor is likely to be the CEO; for a change program designed for a business unit or division, the sponsor will likely be the head of that unit or division. In many change programs, governance cascades down the organization, so some divisions have their own sponsor and PMO for their portions of the program. The sponsor has ultimate responsibility for achieving and sustaining the transformation that the program was designed for.

The sponsor is frequently supported by a steering committee, which might be a group of senior leaders convened for this purpose or the senior leadership team of the organization or business unit. The senior leaders involved will help guide and shape the program and might, individually, be accountable for specific parts of it. Among their tasks are energizing initiative leaders and participants, listening to feedback, removing roadblocks, ensuring sufficient resourcing, helping initiative leaders recognize and resolve problems early on, and rewarding the workforce when milestones are met.

The sponsor empowers the PMO and initiative leaders, and checks that the PMO is fully aligned with his or her vision so that the governance team as a whole speaks with one voice and is clearly seen as unified. Sponsors must take care to provide the right level of input and they should find sufficient energy and time for the program.

The PMO oversees the program operationally, ensuring that each initiative is properly chartered, resourced, and organized for success. As the steward of value, the PMO promotes cooperation across the organization in support of the change program. It helps to bring all initiatives into alignment, monitors progress, and keeps the sponsor and senior leaders informed so that they can take action promptly when needed. When issues arise, the PMO makes sure that the appropriate conversations occur and that initiative leaders understand their accountabilities and are equipped to implement them.

The PMO leader might be involved in the design of the overall program and in choosing the blend of initiatives best able to achieve the program's goals.

Executional Certainty

Given the complexity of large-scale change programs, senior leaders face a tough challenge in overseeing them and guiding them to success. Organizations can overcome that challenge through executional certainty – a set of activities aimed at providing senior leaders with a clear grasp of each initiative's purpose, operational insights, and regular progress reports. Rather than hearing the dreaded words, "There's an issue that's been simmering for some time . . ." senior leaders can identify issues early and resolve them promptly. A set of tactics and tools to accomplish this responsiveness has been developed and refined over the past 20 years and has been embraced by organizations around the world.

Broadly, the activities are as follows: assessing upfront the design of the initiatives and the way that the teams are constituted; maximizing understanding of the key milestones and intended impacts; and providing forward-looking indicators that will prompt timely course corrections. To avoid overburdening the senior leaders, the activities should be carried out with *minimum sufficiency* – for instance, only the most critical information is reported to the senior leaders, giving them an overview of progress and equipping them to act quickly and decisively. Various tools are available for facilitating executional certainty, such as Rigor Testing, Rigorous Program Management (RPM), and DICE: project *duration*, performance *integrity*, *commitment* of executives and staff, and *effort* to cope with change.[11]

DICE provides a means of assessing the prospects and risks inherent in any change effort; it uses empirical precedent to evaluate each initiative's team selection, overall work plan, and other success factors.[12] Rigor Testing is a process for gauging the robustness and consistency of a proposed initiative by testing the clarity and specificity of its plans. RPM ensures efficient tracking and reporting of the progress of a program, and helps guide senior leaders' decisions. In other words, it reinforces their organizational power with operational insights. Regular progress reports enable senior leaders to affirm and encourage when things are going well and to make course corrections when things are going wrong. A crucial component of RPM is the initiative roadmap, which characterizes each initiative by listing the essentials: 5 to 20 milestones, the main risks and interdependencies, and early-warning indicators. The roadmap is a statement of the initiative's targets and the main measures required for reaching them. It keeps the initiative team focused and motivated, and it clarifies accountability so that all participants feel the consequences of their actions promptly – a key tenet of Smart Simplicity.

---

11 DICE includes patented technology (US Patent 8,818,756) and patent pending technology. The name is a registered trademark of The Boston Consulting Group.

12 For further information on DICE scores and the predictive powers of DICE, see, for example, Harold L. Sirkin, Perry Keenan, and Alan Jackson, "The Hard Side of Change Management," *Harvard Business Review*, October 2005.

In general, executional certainty ensures that the change program is set up for success from the start and applies the first and most fundamental rule of Smart Simplicity – *understand what people actually do* – to monitor progress and identify the changes in behavior that would get initiatives back on track.

Enabled Leaders

Even though a change program is initiated and sponsored by the company's top leadership team, the real driving force is the extended leadership team, fully aligned and activated. The extended leadership team consists typically of the CEO, the CEO's direct reports, their direct reports, and select layer 4 and layer 5 managers. In a large organization, the team might, as mentioned earlier, consist of the top 150 senior managers. These individuals on the extended team are crucial for overseeing the program to completion; and because of their proximity to employees, they are also in the best position to engage the full workforce in meeting the program's goals and to secure buy-in from the entire organization. Employees generally respond better to their immediate or near-immediate supervisors than to more-distant senior leaders, since it is these proximate supervisors who influence most strongly the stakes that matter to employees, such as project assignments, performance reviews, and opportunities for advancement.

To be properly enabled, the members of this extended leadership team need to have a vested interest in the program's success. They should also be aligned in their views on how to attain that success; again, they should speak with one voice. They must be committed to the program, be eager to own and lead it, and be responsible for its results. Duly empowered and included early on, they will exercise their power to garner support for the program among the broader organization – by ensuring in turn that it's in each employee's individual interest to participate fully.

Engaged Organization

An engaged organization is one that is motivated and equipped to support the change effort. A change program relies crucially on the buy-in of employees, so the program must be designed in such a way that they are willing and able to adopt their assigned roles and to complete their specified workload – willing, because it's now in their best interests to comply; and able, because they now possess the requisite tools, information, and power. (Skills building might be required, but that, too, can increase employees' engagement.) More broadly, in keeping with the tenets of Smart Simplicity, the design of the program should aim to create a context for employees that makes it rational for them to actively help the program succeed.

The starting point in creating and maintaining employee engagement is thoughtful and effective communication. All participants, at every level, need to understand clearly the program's rationale and design, its role in driving the organization's strategy, and their own roles and responsibilities within the program. The messages may need to be repeated and reinforced regularly. Even a brilliantly designed change program will likely founder if participants remain uninformed or unconvinced of its virtues.[13] Finally, since communication involves listening, not just talking, the messages should be bidirectional; that is, they should not only cascade down the organization but also flow upward, with feedback collected regularly, to ensure transparency and resolve emerging issues before they become obstacles.

An engaged organization is all the more important now, in light of the growing millennial and generation Z presence in the workforce. Generally speaking, these employees seek greater meaning from their work than their pre-millennial counterparts did – and they are more amenable to job mobility. With their skill sets and aspirations, they expect to have some input or at least insight into senior management's key decisions and will readily change jobs if they feel marginalized. The new norm in organizations, both in regular times and in times of change, is greater openness, better communication, and increased employee involvement in decisions.

The Four Elements in Concert

Bear in mind that the four elements of the Change Delta depend heavily on one another. Jointly, they bring energy and clearer accountability to the delivery of the change program. If all four elements are working optimally, several happy outcomes emerge: operational insight is maximized; people feel that they are being treated respectfully, and the leaders and lines are engaged actively and harmoniously; the overall effort is pursued with consistency,

---

13 A useful guideline here is the rule of "three and nine": during a time of major change, leaders should communicate three times more than seems instinctively reasonable, in order to drive the message home; and employees usually need to hear the message nine times for them to fully accept that it relates to them and to understand what it means for them.

with rigor, and ultimately with success; and foundations are laid for even bolder change in the future.

Farewell to the Fatal Errors

Suppose that the companies in the case studies cited earlier had all recognized the shortcomings of their initial attempts and had turned to Smart Simplicity and the Change Delta for help in approaching their change programs. In that alternative world, things would have worked out very differently.

Smart Solution 1: Making Participation Individually Rewarding

The industrial goods company had a serious challenge on its hands. When appeals to the common interest failed to work, leadership resolved to find an explanation for the forecasters' persistence in making overly conservative forecasts. Clearly they must have had some motive for doing so – some rationale grounded in their individual interests. An investigation concluded that matters would not improve as long as the forecasters remained in the commercial division, with their futures dependent on positive feedback there, and as long as the manufacturing team perceived a much larger downside to stockouts than to excess inventory.

Armed with this new understanding, the executives sponsoring the change program began afresh. They again formulated a cogent case for change and publicized the collective benefits, but this time they arranged some changes of their own: henceforward, the forecasting team would report to a business support team – which provided services to the commercial and manufacturing divisions but did not report directly to either of them – and would be assessed and rewarded for accuracy. The business support team would regularly check the sales forecasts to ensure that they reflected expected business growth and would encourage the forecasting team to adopt the latest, most sophisticated methods. Moreover, the manufacturing team, while still being held accountable for stockouts, would also be accountable for the carrying costs of excess inventory. Sure enough, the forecasters and manufacturing team began to view things differently: the forecasters found conservative forecasting to be less attractive than before, and they now had a personal incentive to move to the new system, while the manufacturing team no longer felt compelled to build in a large buffer.

Smart Solution 2: Extensively Engaging the Extended Leadership Team

The senior executives of the bank reviewed their previous, failed efforts at promoting cultural change and determined to redesign the program. This time, there would be an emphasis on getting the extended leadership team involved and aligned with the change program as early as possible. The program's sponsors organized a comprehensive communication and enablement package, including a two-day leadership summit and face-to-face follow-up meetings, to clarify the purpose of the transformation and listen to participants' concerns and suggestions. The extended leadership team explained, for instance, why current, damaging practices persisted (why the practices were a rational choice for the loan officers) and debated how the sponsors might change the program (in order to make the new, favorable practices rational instead). The extended leadership team also explained to the senior leaders the serious mismatch that the current system permitted: the loan officers who made numerous high-interest loans received higher bonuses, earned greater respect, and gained promotion faster, regardless of how risky the loans were, whereas the impact of the associated risk (in terms of failed loans) took years to hit the books – by which point many of the loan officers had moved to other positions or other companies.

The senior leaders were now in a position to make several organization-wide modifications aimed at reducing the appeal of excessively risky behavior. They implemented an incentive system for the loan officers that penalized rather than rewarded those who took extravagant risks. They also reinforced the extended leadership team's determination to reduce risk: they rallied the team's leadership instincts by warning that a persistently risky loan portfolio could lead to layoffs among the staff, and they offered the team a bonus if the risk of the portfolio decreased to an acceptable level.

The members of the extended leadership team, having been engaged early on and properly empowered, felt that they owned the change agenda and were the right people to see it through. Their commitment was intense, both through being at the front lines and through realizing that their own success was linked to the success of the program. They communicated to their teams the new vision for the company, coached individual employees on new behaviors, and enhanced the change program by removing obstacles.

Their strong engagement cascaded down to the sales teams and individual loan officers. It could not have come at a better time: the industry was going through a particularly troubled phase. The company was nevertheless able to deliver impressively on almost all aspects of the change program, not only weathering the storm but emerging in far better shape than before, having shifted the portfolio to a less risky and longer-term customer base.

Smart Solution 3: Empowering the PMO

At the oil and gas company, senior executives agreed that if the productivity transformation was to make good, it needed a "PMO with teeth." An underpowered PMO would be unable to corral the initiative leaders, who would instead persist in focusing on their day-to-day duties. During the planning stages, senior leaders put a lot of thought into the ideal setup for the PMO – its reporting relationship with them, its mandate, and its resourcing. The PMO was now assigned the requisite authority, was duly anointed as a steward of value in support of senior leadership, and was staffed by up-and-coming, high-potential leaders who would report directly to an influential member of the executive team.

One notable achievement of the PMO was shaping how initiative leaders thought of risk and reported it to the senior leadership team. In keeping with standard practice, the PMO helped them analyze risk-based information and use it in setting milestones; but the PMO also went one step further, asking initiative leaders to describe the risks most likely to derail each project and to suggest the leading indicators of these risks. For instance, in an initiative aimed at building up capability for assessing geological sites to acquire, a leading indicator was the number of attractive candidates applying for the technical roles. When it emerged that insufficient high-quality candidates were applying, senior leadership was able to intervene promptly and hire specialist recruiters to help bridge the talent gap.

With the backing of senior leadership, the PMO was willing and able to coordinate the units involved, promote cooperation across lines, and drive the program to success. Note that the PMO's charter was not to usurp but to facilitate the work of the initiative leaders, raise issues on behalf of senior leadership, and alert executives promptly to any intractable problems.

The initiative leaders accorded the PMO a grudging respect and ended up cooperating beyond the minimum specifications: they offered valuable operational insights, adjusted their focus in order to harmonize with other initiatives, spontaneously raised early concerns about hitting targets, and put forward their own ideas for course correction.

Smart Solution 4: Effectively Defining and Tracking Progress

The credit card company's new CEO was respectful of the federated corporate structure that she had inherited, but she made it clear to department leaders that their cost reduction efforts would now be checked and reported by the PMO, backed by the steering committee – though just enough to foresee major risks and allow for corrections. Heartened by this relatively hands-off approach, the department leaders agreed to various changes: they would develop and apply forward-looking metrics, they would cooperate fully with the PMO in rigor testing the change initiatives, and they would ensure transparency on the issues that particularly concerned senior management. In addition, they would lend their support to developing a number of cross-department initiatives.

The CEO reassured them that the PMO would not weaken their authority or threaten their autonomy: the reason for the PMO's increased involvement was the complexity of the change program, in particular the many cross-functional dependencies involved. As the CEO put it, effective oversight had to be implemented in order to give senior leadership the necessary operational insights and the means to intervene and suggest course corrections early enough to make a difference. In general, the change program would be wielding a scalpel, not a jackhammer.

During the design phase of the program, the PMO stress tested the initiatives – their risks, likely financial impact, and realistic milestones – which were duly incorporated into the final version of the program. The PMO also instituted a monthly meeting at which department heads shared ideas for identifying and changing unproductive behaviors among their staff, and discussed opportunities for cross-department cooperation that would increase productivity. The CEO took to attending these meetings and publicly recognizing bold suggestions; in due course, the department heads who could not propose creative, cooperative solutions were perceived by their peers to be letting the program down.

The effect was as much preventive as curative. The department managers – appreciative rather than resentful of the coordination effort – strove to reach each milestone punctually. When things deviated from the roadmap, the PMO was alerted promptly and initiated early course corrections. The PMO took care to consult the relevant team leaders about the best intervention and let them take the lead in getting back on track. The department leaders, even while working intently at meeting their monthly targets, were motivated to look beyond their silos and beyond the short term and contribute to a sustainable, company-wide performance boost.

Changing for the Better

The Change Delta, with Smart Simplicity at its core, has proved its potency time and again. Companies around the world have benefited from it, averaging 110% of targeted performance improvements across a range of challenging and complex change programs. Compare that with the industry average of 50% to 75% failure rates (with the more complex programs registering the lower scores).

What about the Future?

As digital technology grows ever more powerful and more widely applied, exploiting it for change management purposes will pose new challenges and opportunities. We expect an increasing shift toward "agile" project delivery approaches and other working models (involving more mobile talent, for example). We also expect even greater employee involvement and an increase in bottom-up input relative to top-down direction. But Smart Simplicity and the Change Delta will remain valid.

Using a set of minimally sufficient but proven approaches, the Change Delta promotes cooperation by aligning people's interests with those of the program as a whole. In doing so, it fulfills the key ambitions of any change program – to bring about *sustainable* improvements in performance (without undue disruption), to enable as many people as possible to experience the change in the most positive way possible, and to build the capability for even bolder change.

By using the Change Delta, and the Smart Simplicity principles on which it is based, organizations will modify the prospects of their change programs for the better, and the change management industry as a whole will live up to its claims and fulfill its potential.

Hans-Paul Bürkner, Lars Fæste, Jim Hemerling, Yulia Lyusina, and Martin Reeves

Chapter 9
The Transformations that Work, and Why

Recently, many global companies – for example, China Petroleum and Coca-Cola – have named new CEOs. In many cases, this was because shareholders or the board felt that the previous leaders did not understand the massive disruptions facing their industries. These are not isolated events. Churn within many industries, due to incessant technological change, now means that leaders are being overtaken by their competitors at an unprecedented pace.[1]

At any one time, about one-third of large US companies are experiencing a severe, two-year decline in their ability to create shareholder value. Within that group, one-third fail to recover within the following five years. Even companies that are current industry leaders are vulnerable to disruption. Even the new leader of a top-performing company needs to watch over their shoulder for – and transform the company in anticipation of – the next disruption, for it is surely coming. In other words, if the company ain't broke, fix it preemptively anyway.

Many new CEOs come in with a mandate to transform the company – including its strategy, business model, organization, operations, and culture. A transformation is not a series of incremental changes. Rather, it is a fundamental reboot that enables a business to achieve a dramatic, sustainable improvement in performance and alter the trajectory of its future. Because they are comprehensive by nature, transformations[2] are complex endeavors, and the majority fall short of expectations for achieving their target value, coming in on time, or doing both.[3]

---

1 See Martin Reeves and Knut Haanæs, *Your Strategy Needs a Strategy*, Harvard Business Review Press, 2015.

2 "What Is Transformation? Transformations have become a global imperative across industries. With disruption now the norm, companies need a solid transformation strategy just to compete in today's increasingly complex and volatile business world," *BCG Capabilities*. https://www.bcg.com/capabilities/transformation/turnaround-restructuring/what-is-transformation [accessed 9/5/2020].

3 See *Transformation: Delivering and Sustaining Breakthrough Performance*, BCG e-book, November 2016.

https://doi.org/10.1515/9783110697834-009

The good news is that changing CEOs increases the odds of success. The bad news is that new CEOs – particularly those hired from outside the company – also show a wide range of success in leading transformations. This chapter summarizes the best practices from direct experience and analysis and offers new CEOs an evidence-based approach for developing and implementing successful transformations.

Transformation Raises the Bar for CEOs

There are several reasons why transformations raise the bar for CEOs – especially those new to the executive position.

- *CEOs must continually balance short- and long-term objectives:* An incoming CEO faces immediate pressure to deliver top-quartile performance in the company's core business, in many cases, through short-term improvements. At the same time, the new CEO must reinvent the business model, enhance product and service offerings, and invest in other long-term initiatives. The best CEOs can do both.
- *CEOs must quickly reset investor expectations:* Within six months of taking over, new CEOs need to evaluate which parts of the business are still viable, identify the most urgently required improvements, and determine where the company's future growth lies. They must not only develop a strong plan – including potentially painful measures to restructure, sell, or close legacy businesses – but must also communicate this plan to their investors.
- *CEOs must develop a clear purpose for the change effort:* At any given time, in this era of always-on transformation, companies have multiple initiatives underway, which can be exhausting for people in the organization as they cope with constant change. CEOs need to reenergize people with an explicit purpose – the "why" around which management and the rest of the organization can rally.
- *CEOs must adopt agile and digital methods to drive change:* To get breakthrough results fast, while inspiring and engaging employees, leaders should adopt agile approaches – for example, mapping customer pain points, establishing cross-functional teams, and establishing new ways of working, such as two-week "sprints," obstacle boards, and minimum viable products. At the same time, they must leverage digital technologies to improve the customer experience and simplify workflows (see the Case Study "A Bank Transforms Through Agile and Digital").

A Bank Transforms through Agile and Digital

The financial services industry is digitizing, and consumers are interacting with their banks in new ways. One bank recently launched a multiyear transformation, starting with the appointment of a new CEO.

The transformation thus far has seen three phases: (1) strategic focus by selling off noncore assets; (2) reliable delivery on commitments to investors through tighter management of revenues, costs, and investments; and (3) the rollout of new processes for consumers, capitalizing on digital and using the agile approach to speed the time to market. All cross-functional teams work in the same space and have a high degree of autonomy and decision-making authority during the product development process.

Rather than taking months or years, rollout of new services can be achieved in weeks, in part because the objective is to get a minimum viable product into the market as soon as possible. From that point, the development team can capture feedback and make rapid design iterations, improving the product.

The company has used several tools to make this happen:
- A 90-day countdown clock that pressures teams to deliver their projects on time
- A visual escalation board that impels action to clear project bottlenecks within 96 hours
- A wall of champions aimed at fostering a competitive spirit and celebrating successes
- An open-door policy that encourages employees to raise issues and express concerns

Through this program, which relies heavily on digital technology, the bank has dramatically accelerated the pace of standard customer processes. Opening a new account, which used to take nine days, now uses a digital approach and takes just 10 minutes. Business transactions that once took six days have been equally accelerated. A virtual self-service business assistant for business customers saves up to $16 million per year.

The program's benefits include higher revenues (as much as 3% higher for selected initiatives), lower costs due to more streamlined and digitized processes, and a superior customer experience with higher customer ratings and conversion levels. Moreover, because teams are now freed to move fast and deliver innovative new offerings, the transformation has enhanced employee satisfaction, engagement, and inspiration.

- *CEOs must assemble diverse leadership teams:* Assembling the right senior executive team, a critical component of transformation success, is a challenge for some CEOs. The ideal team includes people from inside and outside the organization who understand the current core business, as well as the actions needed in order to respond to – or lead – disruptive change. It is important to strike the right balance between external hires (who can bring fresh ideas and new capabilities, particularly digital) and internal talent (who know the business and organization).
- *CEOs need to apply directive and inclusive leadership*: Leaders cannot simply set the broad vision for a transformation and then delegate its execution.

Instead, they must show directive leadership, setting the ambition, articulating strategic priorities, and holding management accountable for results. At the same time, they need to be inclusive, involving their teams early on, fostering collaboration, soliciting honest feedback, and empowering teams to define and implement specific initiatives. Striking this balance can be difficult, especially during the intense pressure of a major transformation effort.

Key Findings from the Analysis

In addition to our first-hand experience with transformations at large companies worldwide, we analyzed transformation programs at large US companies to determine key success factors. Our analysis focused on companies that had shown a dramatic decline in total shareholder return.

The findings offer some evidence-based guidance for new CEOs:

- *Virtually every company needs a transformation:* Roughly one-third of the companies we analyzed had faced a sharp decline (more than 10 percentage points) in total shareholder return (TSR) over any two-year span. Within that subset, one-third had deteriorated even more over the following five years. The clear implication is that most companies need to transform at least once during any five-year window. And given the fact that transformations are multiple-year endeavors, they inevitably overlap.

- *Some predictable factors separate winners from losers:* Some factors have a significant impact on the long-term results of a transformation. Specifically, companies that invest more in R&D and have a long-term strategic outlook are the most likely to post outsize gains in TSR following a transformation. This is partly because companies that deliver a cogent plan to investors gain credibility, which leads to higher expectations and valuation multiples. Similarly, hiring a new CEO, particularly one from outside the company, has a positive impact, and companies that have a formal transformation program in place – rather than a series of ad hoc improvements – perform best (Figure 9.1). Moreover, these factors work together: building a transformation around all three aspects can increase a company's long-term TSR by 13.5 percentage points.

- *In setting a long-term strategy, revenue growth is the biggest factor in transformation success:* Meeting expectations in the early stages establishes credibility, and costs are important across all time periods; but over the long term, increases in sales have the greatest impact on shareholder value.

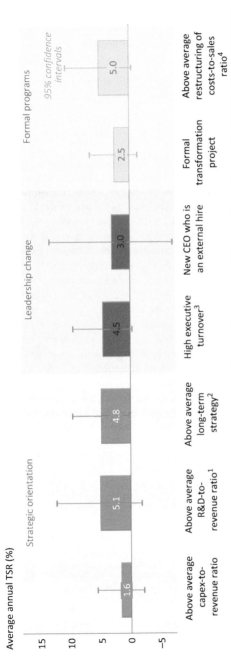

Figure 9.1: Three Factors That Lead to Long-Term Transformation Success.

A company can't cut and trim its way to top-quartile performance. Transformation requires balancing the opposing aims of cost discipline and investment in the future. Notably, investments in capital expenditures do not automatically lead to improved performance. Instead, companies should aim to grow by spending on R&D with a clear link to sales growth (see the Case Study "Carlsberg Saves $300 Million and Reinvests for Growth").

Carlsberg Saves $300 Million and Reinvests for Growth

Carlsberg, a 170-year-old global consumer goods company, had been stagnating for several years, owing to heavy debt and challenging market conditions. The company's sales volumes were declining in several markets, and EBIT margins trailed behind those of its competitors.

In 2015, Cees 't Hart joined the company as CEO with the forceful idea of a strategic transformation aimed at restoring growth, focusing on premium products, and reorienting the company toward more attractive market segments. The company's considerable debt burden complicated the challenge, but Hart addressed that by launching a comprehensive two-year program. The goal was to save approximately $300 million and reinvest half of that in strategic measures that would boost growth, employee engagement, and new capabilities.

The transformation had two key components to fund the journey. First, Carlsberg reduced costs by streamlining the organization, improving operations, and increasing the efficiency of production processes. Procurement measures led to additional savings, as did steps to reduce complexity. Next, the company boosted short-term revenue growth by adjusting its mix of products, optimizing revenue management, and applying a systematic lens to promotions.

In addition, Hart set out to reconnect with Carlsberg's original purpose so that the organization could draw strength from its foundation and heritage.

This comprehensive approach allowed the company to reduce debt significantly, raise EBIT margins, and position itself to invest in the future. The share price shot up during the first two years, reaching an all-time high and – in terms of shareholder returns – beating Carlsberg's main peers.

- *On average, new CEOs hired externally show better – but also greater variation in – performance than internal hires:* Many outsider CEOs bring a new perspective to a company's situation. Because they may not have much tied up in the success of previous approaches, they are more willing to make dramatic changes. As a result, outsider CEOs typically lead to better TSR than those hired internally. The caveat, however, is that the results of outsider CEOs also show greater variability (Figure 9.2). These CEOs take big swings, which sometimes lead to home runs but can also lead to strikeouts. A company needs, therefore, to be mindful of the potential for variability if it is recruiting from outside the company.

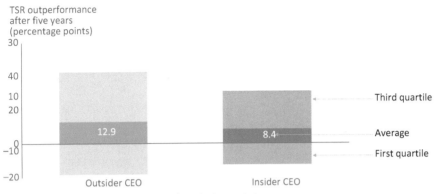

TSR outperformance
after five years
(percentage points)

Sources: Capital IQ; Thomson; Edgar; BCG Henderson Institute analysis

Figure 9.2: Outsider CEOs Have More Successful Transformations But a Wider Range of Performance.

- *Rapid action will be rewarded:* Finally, new CEOs need to understand the urgency of their company's situation and take rapid action. We have found that some new CEOs are cautious about taking quick action and hesitate to make changes that go deep enough to make a difference. Developing and communicating a clear plan to investors can establish the CEO's credibility and lead to the biggest short-term difference in performance – an increase in the valuation multiple. The message for incoming leaders is clear: you must show compelling plans and take immediate action. By laying the groundwork in advance, you can be prepared to lead from the front with a clear vision, solid objectives, and the tools and processes to succeed.

A Four-Part Approach

On the basis of our experience helping companies design and implement transformations, as well as the findings of our quantitative analysis, we have identified four transformation imperatives for new CEOs: (1) prepare the journey, (2) fund the journey, (3) reinvent for the future, and (4) organize for sustained performance (Figure 9.3).

Prepare the journey

- Analyze the company's situation; talk with internal and external stakeholders
- Assess disruption, understand new entrants and new business models
- Assess the organization's adaptability and readiness for change
- Develop a formal, structured transformation program
- Articulate a clear purpose for the transformation, and communicate it clearly and continually

Fund the journey

- Shift from planning the transformation to leading it
- Develop no-regret initiatives that can generate results within 3 to 12 months
- In addition to reducing costs and simplifying the organization, launch measures to boost revenues and improve capital efficiency
- Establish agile teams and build an agile culture for certain projects
- Implement digital quick wins to build up institutional expertise

Reinvent for the future

- Plan, develop, and launch broader initiatives to boost innovation, revenue growth, and long-term value creation (focus on R&D, commercial operations, new ventures)
- Assess and re-define the company's overall strategy and operating model
- Adopt a "self-disruption" mindset, aggressively using digital to mitigate external threats and create new opportunities
- Start implementing new tools such has data analytics

Organize for sustained performance

- Ensure that the executive team has the right commitment and change management capabilities
- Simplify the organization and culture to sustain high performance
- Build a talent pipeline to fill crucial roles
- Install an HR team that can act as a transformation partner
- Deploy change management tools and processes to engage stakeholders and deliver results

Figure 9.3: CEO's Four-Part Transformation Process.

Source: BCG analysis

Prepare the Journey

Before a new CEO takes over, and during the first few weeks on the job, he or she needs to take charge, develop a clear-eyed view of the company's current situation, and define the organization's collective transformation ambition.

In defining this ambition, it is critically important for CEOs – whether hired from within or brought in from outside – to adopt an investigative and analytical mindset that says, "I need to learn more." Incoming leaders should talk with as many critical stakeholders as possible, including employees, customers, and industry and functional experts, to educate themselves about the company. This also includes identifying and talking with new entrants and startups in the company's business and adjacent businesses and offering speed and new alternative business models. Ideally, to be able to move quickly, a new CEO should gather the new leadership team even before getting started. Then, it's important to establish a management meeting cadence and meet frequently to ensure that everybody is on board.

Most important, the transformation should be structured as a formal program. Rather than business as usual or a few incremental measures, this program should bring profound change that has the potential to affect the entire organization and that aims to improve performance substantially. Such a program requires flexibility that allows leaders to revisit the plan and make adjustments on an ongoing basis.

During the initial weeks and months of a new CEO's tenure, communication is critical for engaging and energizing the company. Leadership transitions and transformations can be stressful periods for any company, and undergoing both simultaneously doubles the pressure: employees must go above and beyond their regular responsibilities, working in unfamiliar – and even initially uncomfortable – ways. The always-on transformation makes this challenge even more difficult, because it removes the finish line. Accordingly, the CEO should articulate, activate, and embed a clear purpose for the work that the company does each day, establishing an explicit link that shows how the transformation supports that purpose. Our research has shown that companies with a strong and clear purpose deliver better financial performance over time.[4] One key reason for this is that bold action and clear communication can help establish credibility with investors and other stakeholders.

---

4 See "Purpose with the Power to Transform Your Organization," *BCG Focus*, May 2017. https://www.bcg.com/publications/2017/transformation-behavior-culture-purpose-power-transform-organization [accessed 9/5/2020].

Fund the Journey

As the transformation starts to take shape and the case for change becomes clear, the CEO must shift gears from planning the transformation to actually leading it. This means immediately kicking off rapid, no-regret moves – initiatives that are relatively easy to implement in the first 100 days and that can generate results in 3 to 12 months. These no-regrets initiatives should close performance gaps in a few critical areas, reduce costs, improve top- and bottom-line performance, and free up cash in order to fuel longer-term initiatives (see the Case Study "A Chinese Industrial Goods Company Transforms Itself to Improve Operations").

A Chinese Industrial Goods Company Transforms Itself to Improve Operations
After a dramatic expansion, a Chinese industrial goods company needed an operational transformation to improve and standardize production. Several of its large plants were losing money on each ton of finished goods. The transformation program combined multiple no-regrets measures aimed at stabilizing the company's situation and transforming the organization, including optimizing the product cost, reducing inventory, standardizing and improving key processes, and revamping services such as handling customer complaints. The program also included growth-oriented measures, such as the launch of new high-end products, more effective coordination among factories to optimize the product mix, and improvements to the customer mix.

At a later stage, the company launched a series of initiatives for building a long-term platform for success, including optimizing logistics and improving quality control.

As a result of the transformation, the company's margins turned positive within two years, and it began to create value as it grew. More impressive, the company embedded the transformation measures into the daily activity of each plant, making the changes sustainable over time.

The primary levers for funding the journey are revenue increases, organizational simplicity (delayering), capital efficiency, and cost reduction – and digital applies across all four levers. In deciding where to start, many companies opt for the obvious solution: cost reduction. We have found that even though revenue and organizational simplicity measures can have an even faster impact, they are often overlooked.

With regard to digitization, small-scale pilot tests and quick wins are crucial to kick-starting transformation – they build up institutional expertise, serve as proofs of concept, and build momentum for broader efforts. Given the dynamic nature of business and the fact that transformations take years to implement, some traditional practices can no longer keep up. Long delivery cycles are no longer viable, especially as agile ways of working become more prevalent. Increasingly, leading companies are using agile methodologies to implement change. Done right, agile requires creating small, nimble, cross-functional teams that have been given a high degree of autonomy. These teams, which can move much faster than traditional organization structures, promote better output, shorter time to market, and higher satisfaction among employees and customers alike.[5]

A new CEO must push hard to get things done. If the team is not performing, the new company leader shouldn't hesitate to remove people quickly.

A Global Industrial Company Wins through a Commercial Transformation Built Around Digital
A large industrial company launched a massive digital transformation aimed at increasing its efficiency and competing more effectively in markets whose producers have limited pricing power. The company did not want to tie up capital in a massive change program and wait years for a payback. To avoid that outcome, the company first identified a few quick-win initiatives that would pay off within a month or a quarter.

It first selected initiatives in inventory management and capacity optimization, analyzing output and shifting production to sites that were the most profitable. For these quick wins, the company used static data and created one-off solutions, but the projects led to significant savings and increasing sales of high-profit items, which generated immediate value.

Within nine months, these initiatives had generated $20 million in value. Once the projects that were based on static data were up and running, the company went back and built the systems it needed for managing these processes and functions continuously, using real-time data flows.

Applying lessons from its early wins, the company created a roadmap for ten major data transformation initiatives in areas such as demand forecasting and sales force management. The company also made plans for new, company-wide resources, including a data repository that will support and sustain data-driven approaches. And it has begun to identify new data-driven business models.

The overall goal for the transformation is to unlock $200 million in value over three to five years and to help the company raise its EBITDA by 2% to 4%.

Reinvent for the Future

In parallel with initial fund-the-journey efforts, the CEO must launch broader initiatives to reinvent the company for the future and build sustainable performance with a focus on innovation, growth, and long-term value creation. Reinventing for the future can entail a wide range of initiatives to transform, including boosting growth, launching a new business model, revamping commercial processes

---

5 See "Taking Agile Way Beyond Software," *BCG article*, July 2017. https://www.bcg.com/publica tions/2017/technology-digital-organization-taking-agile-way-beyond-software [accessed 9/5/2020].

or operations, building digital capabilities and ventures, and transforming critical processes, such as R&D, and internal support functions, such as IT and HR.

Nokia Reprograms Itself for Growth

Nokia, which has transformed itself – in a range of industries and products – many times in its 150-year history, didn't settle on phones and networking equipment until the 1980s, when mobile technology took off. In 2007, the company dominated the mobile phone space, owning 40% of the global market, thanks to clearly superior technology and enormous advantages of scale. Just five years later, however, Nokia was in a severe crisis: market capitalization was 96% lower than it had been in 2007, it was burning cash, and its operating losses exceeded $2 billion in the first six months of 2012 alone.

In response, Nokia launched a dramatic, bet-the-company turnaround. The top strategic concern was the fate of its mobile phone business. In the war of the mobile ecosystems, Apple's iOS and Google's Android were rapidly capturing larger and larger chunks of the smartphone market, and it seemed unlikely that Nokia's Windows Phone strategy would be able to save the company. So Nokia decided to sell its mobile phone business to Microsoft and announced the divestment as part of a $7.2 billion deal in September 2013.

After the divestment, the new Nokia was essentially a portfolio of three fairly different businesses: network infrastructure, mapping services, and technology and patent licensing. This situation brought Nokia to its next big strategic decision. Should the company start to develop itself as a portfolio company or should it focus its activities?

Nokia's largest remaining operational unit was the network business, but since 2007, Nokia had been operating its network infrastructure unit as a 50-50 joint venture with Siemens. Until 2013, Nokia had been planning to reduce its involvement in the business by preparing the joint venture for a full spinoff and IPO.

As a first move toward building a stronger presence in this industry, Nokia decided to take full control of this unit by buying out Siemens. Why? The joint venture agreement was coming to an end, and one of the parties would need to assume full ownership – along with all the associated risks and rewards. Nokia's move proved a success: over the next two years, the company successfully integrated the network unit as the new core of the corporation, generating several billion dollars in shareholder value.

However, the full extent of Nokia's grand plan for the network infrastructure business was revealed only two years later. In 2015, Nokia announced its intent to acquire Alcatel-Lucent. With this industry-shaping $16.6 billion acquisition, Nokia expanded its business from being a provider of mobile network services to covering the full range of products and services in network infrastructure (such as IP routing and optical networks). Furthermore, it strengthened its presence in North America. During the same year, Nokia sharpened its focus by divesting its mapping business to a group of German car companies (including Audi, BMW, and Daimler) for $3 billion.

Despite its repositioning as a full-fledged network infrastructure provider, Nokia decided to retain its patent- and technology-licensing business in order to sustain its legacy of innovation and reinvention. In addition to holding the majority of Nokia's patents, the unit today innovates in such areas as virtual reality and digital health. Although it accounted for less than 5% of Nokia's 2016 revenues, the unit generated 22% of the operating profits and, according to analysts, an even higher share of the group valuation.

To understand how drastically Nokia has changed in the course of its journey, one can look at Nokia's workforce. Since the start of the turnaround through early 2017, the company had turned over 99% of the employee base, 80% of the board of directors, and all but one member of the executive team. Chairman Risto Siilasmaa, who took over in May 2012 at the height of Nokia's troubles, described the journey: "It has been a complete removal of engines, the cabin, and the wings of an airplane and reassembling the airplane to look very different."

This transformation – from walking dead to thriving in a new core business – won't likely be Nokia's last. But its success shows that the company can navigate massive disruptions, reorient itself, and come back ever stronger. Today, Nokia is once again the pride of Finland: the nation's most valuable company, Nokia is well positioned for the next chapter in its long history.

While they are driving transformation initiatives, companies benefit from stepping back and reviewing their overall strategy and operating model. As discussed above, the best path to long-term value creation is a sharp focus on increasing revenues in the core business through targeted R&D investments that can unlock growth to fund future initiatives.

A New CEO Transforms a Pharmaceutical Company

When a new CEO took over a large pharmaceutical business, he quickly realized that pressures in the health care industry, intensifying competition, and the company's evolving product portfolio meant that the company would require a transformation.

Accordingly, the leadership team developed a new operating model configured to incorporate the following features:

- Customer interactions designed to optimize the patient experience
- An agile, technology-enabled infrastructure that frees resources for strategic investments
- A new HR strategy to improve employees' engagement and better assess their performance
- Clear governance with minimal decision-making layers, particularly regarding the company's R&D pipeline
- Greater transparency into the company's deployment of resources to ensure that the focus remains on the products with the biggest potential impact

The transformation has meant dramatically improving financial performance and outpacing competitors in terms of shareholder value creation.

Digital technology is a crucial element of reinventing for the future. Disruptions to most industries are the result of new technology, and the attacks, which seem to arise from nowhere, progress very quickly. Companies need to stay ahead of this threat by disrupting themselves and taking an aggressive approach to implementing digital. Successfully integrating digital not only mitigates threats but also creates opportunities. New tools such as data analytics can dramatically improve a company's financial and operational performance, and other tools open up new value streams.

Organize for Sustained Performance

Transformations are no longer one-time initiatives. Because the pace of change is so fast, companies need to adopt an always-on transformation mindset. Transformations require changing the way that the company operates and, consequently, assembling new talent and capabilities.

The CEO, in conjunction with the leadership team and HR, must determine how the transformation will affect its people, in particular through leadership and talent requirements, organization design changes, new capabilities that need to be developed, and changes in the culture. This process needs to be at the core of the transformation plan from the beginning – this is not an issue that executives can address later in the process.

The imperatives of organizing for sustained performance include the following:

- Ensure that members of the leadership team are capable of heading the transformation in a way that is directive and inclusive. They need to set the appropriate priorities, make rapid, high-quality decisions, mobilize and energize initiative teams, engage the broader organization, and hold themselves accountable for the results.
- Adopt a people-first approach to change, deploying change management approaches, tools, and processes – including, for example, an activist project management office, agile ways of working, high-touch engagement, and digital "nudges" – to engage stakeholders and deliver results.[6]
- Enhance the culture, aligned with the company's purpose, by determining which values and behaviors are required in the transformed organization, and take the actions required to reinforce these values and behaviors as a new way of working. This should happen in conjunction with actions that simplify the organization. Usually, this entails eliminating waste and low-value work, trimming bureaucracy, implementing shared services, automating processes, and enabling the organization to continue taking these steps on an ongoing basis.

---

6 See "Digital-Era Change Runs on People Power," *BCG article*, August 2017. https://www.bcg.com/publications/2017/change-management-organization-digital-era-change-runs-people-power [accessed 9/5/2020].

A Transformation Helps a Software Firm become more Agile

As the market shifted to cloud and mobile offerings, a large software company with a strong legacy business was struggling to capitalize on new growth opportunities. The company's new CEO, realizing that the culture – long a source of strength – might be holding it back, initiated a transformation to make the company more agile and innovative, without increasing costs.

The company launched an 18-month transformation that was based on a broad range of initiatives, including rethinking the portfolio, improving innovation, revamping the corporate function, speeding go-to-market processes, and developing the right talent to support new behaviors. It shifted investments dramatically from legacy to emerging businesses, and it introduced measures to reduce operational costs.

A C-suite-level transformation office, led by the CEO, regularly communicated with project teams to define clear solutions and secure the board's quick approval to expedite and accelerate the progress of ideas from creation to implementation.

The payoff was dramatic: the company identified more than $1 billion in annual cost reductions that it redeployed to high-priority businesses, innovations, and shareholder returns. Furthermore, it emerged with a new engineering model for getting products and services from the design stage to customers rapidly. An improved culture also prioritized innovation while retaining the critical subcultures within certain business lines and functions that employees prized. In all, the company became far more agile and responsive, allowing it to regain its position as a technology market leader.

- Identify talent needs and build a pipeline that can help fill crucial roles, along with developing capabilities in areas critical to the transformation, such as digital, innovation, agile, go-to-market strategies, pricing, sourcing, and lean methods.
- Empower and equip the HR team to act as a transformation partner that anticipates and addresses leadership and talent needs, supports organization redesign, and partners with leaders to develop the culture.

Even large and successful companies need to transform themselves in response to current or looming threats. CEOs need to adopt a mindset of restlessness and continuous change. By following a clear methodology for transformation, starting even before the first day on the job, a new CEO can take the steps needed to make the company more adaptive and responsive, putting it on the right trajectory for success. The best response to external disruption is not playing defense. Rather it is embracing preemptive self-disruption.

Hans-Paul Bürkner, Lars Fæste, and Jim Hemerling

Chapter 10
The New CEO's Guide to Transformation

Leadership transitions increasingly happen when companies are at an inflection point, and as a result, new CEOs frequently face immediate pressure to make changes. The challenges are significant. Companies are being buffeted by rapidly evolving technology and digitization, increasing globalization, blurred industry boundaries, and regulatory shifts, among other factors. As the traditional sources of competitive advantage disappear, top-performing companies are increasing their lead on poor and average performers (Figure 10.1).

To keep up with industry leaders – or to remain a leader – it is more important than ever for companies to undergo transformations.[1] We define a transformation as a profound change in a company's strategy, business model, organization, culture, people, or processes. A transformation is not an incremental change but a fundamental reboot that enables a business to achieve a sustainable, quantum improvement in performance, altering the trajectory of its future. Because of the comprehensive nature of transformations and the need for companies to implement them quickly, transformations are complex endeavors, and the majority either fail to fully capture the potential value or exceed the time allotted to embed new behaviors and processes. Yet by adopting a clear methodology, companies can flip the odds in their favor.

Companies with stable management teams can also benefit from transformations, yet in our experience, a change in leadership offers a critical window of opportunity for implementation. Stakeholders *expect* changes to occur when a new CEO is hired. In fact, a principal risk for new CEOs is that they may resist taking action too quickly – or hesitate to make changes that go deep enough. The risk is especially high for insiders who are being promoted to the top spot or taking the reins alongside a strong chairperson. Yet through quick and decisive actions – even before taking the top job – new CEOs can seize the opportunity and put their company on the right trajectory for success.

---

1 See *Transformation: The Imperative to Change*, BCG report, November 2014. https://www.bcg.com/publications/2014/people-organization-transformation-imperative-change [accessed 9/5/2020].

https://doi.org/10.1515/9783110697834-010

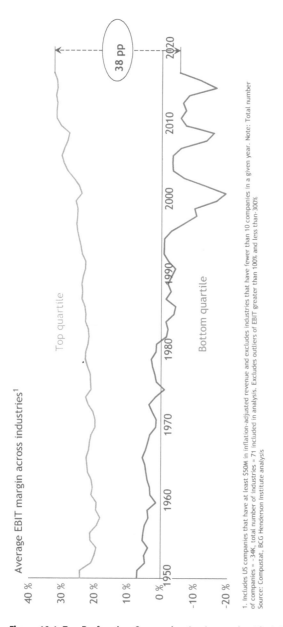

Figure 10.1: Top Performing Companies Are Increasing Their Lead on Poor Performers.

The message for incoming leaders is clear: you need to take action immediately. By laying the groundwork in advance, you can be prepared to lead from the front with a clear vision, solid objectives, and the tools and processes to succeed.

This chapter is a playbook for new CEOs. It lays out how and where to start and provides a transformation framework. The chapter then breaks the transformation process into four steps: (1) the 100 days before officially starting, (2) the first weeks on the job, (3) the first 100 days, and (4) the first 18 months. Because the framework applies to all transformations, while the four steps provide specific actions for new CEOs, there is some overlap. This chapter also includes case studies of successful transformations in various industries – retail, technology, and manufacturing, among others – to show what the process looks like in the real world.

The Transformation Framework

This section describes a framework that can help leaders define the collective transformation ambition for the company (Figure 10.2). The framework has three critical components:

1. *Funding the Journey.* Launch short-term, no-regret moves to establish momentum and to free up capital to fuel new growth engines.
2. *Winning in the Medium Term.* Develop a business model and operating model to increase competitive advantage.
3. *Building the Right Team, Organization, and Culture.* Set up the organization for sustainable high performance.

A transformation should include all three elements, but the relative importance of these components changes at various points in the process. In the beginning, funding the journey is often the most critical aspect, not only to establish momentum but also to free up capital rapidly. Over time, as a transformation takes root, the priorities typically shift toward winning in the medium term. Throughout a transformation, a focus on building the right team, organization, and culture is vital to ensuring that a transformation is not short-lived but rather becomes a long-term endeavor that delivers – and sustains – improved performance.

Funding the journey	Winning in the medium term
• Launch short-term, no-regret moves to create momentum and free up capital • Simplify the organization • Increase capital efficiency • Reduce costs	• Establish the strategic direction for growth • Revamp the business model • Develop a new target operating model • Implement end-to-lean

Building the right team, organization, and culture

• Ensure that the senior management team is leading from the front
• Deploy change management to ensure that people are ready, willing, and able to change
• Install a human resources team that can act as a transformation partner
• Identify and develop talent to fill the critical roles required to transform
• Develop a culture to support high performance

Source: BCG analysis

Figure 10.2: Transformation Framework Components.

One Hundred Days Before Starting: Define the Ambition

New CEOs often have time – as much as 100 days – after unwinding themselves from most of the responsibilities of their former job and before they must assume those of the new position. This period offers a critical opportunity for leaders to take charge and define the organization's collective transformation ambition (Figure 10.3).

When defining this ambition, it is critically important for CEOs – whether hired from the inside or brought in from the outside – to adopt an investigative and analytical mind-set: "I need to learn more." Incoming leaders should talk with as many critical stakeholders as possible, both inside and outside the organization, in order to educate themselves about the company:

- *Employees*, to determine if there is a consensus regarding the changes that are needed; ideally, leaders should speak with 30 to 50 employees from across all units and at all levels
- *Customers*, to get unvarnished opinions of the company's performance in addressing their needs
- *Industry and functional experts*, to understand the company and the complexities or disruptions in the market

Define the ambition	Energize the organization	Prepare and launch the transformation	Drive the transformation
One hundred days before starting	First week	First 100 days	First 18 months
• Analyze a company's situation; talk with internal and external stakeholders • Assess the organization's mind-set and the urgency of the various situations • Develop initial hypotheses on value-creating improvements and identify potential no-regret moves • Assess the leadership team • Plan the first 100 days	• Establish the case for change, discussing external and internal factors • Ensure that the board and senior leadership are in agreement and can "speak with one voice" • Shift to a transformation mind-set, with a clear bias for action • Engage with employees about how ready, willing, and able they are to change	• Develop a roadmap of no-regret initiatives for the transformation; include clear milestones • Create initiatives teams, with charters, resources, plans, and processes • Set up governance, including an activist PMO • Launch the communications plan	• Ensure the delivery of short-term results • Plan, develop, and launch broader initiatives for winning in the medium term • Set new, overall strategy and operating models • Develop the right team, organization and culture to deliver sustainable performance

Note: PMO=program management office
Source: BCG analysis

Figure 10.3: Transformation Process for New CEOs Has Four Stages.

A New Retail CEO Hits the Ground Running

A new CEO was hired to run a retail organization that had been losing market share for several years and that was starting to see profitability decline. During the 100 days before taking over, the CEO visited stores, talked with customers, studied international best practices to build on his own experience abroad, and talked with experts in the retail sector. Through that process, he realized that the immediate priority was to identify rapid, no-regret moves that could increase top-line sales and reenergize the organization.

While conducting this due diligence, the new CEO also developed a strong presentation to introduce his plan to the organization. As soon as he took over, he gave the presentation during the first executive-committee meeting, supporting the plan with the customer feedback he'd generated firsthand, along with his international experience with retail peers. In this presentation, he used very direct language and simple terminology, which made the messages powerful, credible, and resonant.

During his first month, the CEO gave similar presentations to larger groups of employees and managers, which provided clarity and reduced anxiety in the organization. He also traveled to meet the extended management team, visited crucial countries, and granted interviews to select media outlets – always with the same clear and consistent messages.

Within the first quarter, the company had begun to roll out several no-regret moves on the basis of his international retail experience and firsthand research, including a loyalty campaign, extended operating hours for a particular store format, and new promotions. The results jump-started top-line growth for the first time in years, leading to subsequent gains in market share. With those gains behind them, employees were more willing to accept the cost cuts and other measures required for the company to become leaner and more agile.

During these conversations, a new CEO should primarily listen, encourage open and honest discussion, and make sure that all possible dynamic factors and all possible solutions are being brought to the forefront. Through this process, the CEO must start to diagnose problems and create hypotheses regarding which aspects of the company require improvement. This means assessing the urgency of the various situations – in terms of both scope and timing – and determining whether the company should seek to transform a specific function, market, or division, or instead undergo a more comprehensive effort that affects multiple areas of the company.

In both broad and narrow transformation efforts, new CEOs need to start identifying rapid, no-regret moves during this time – initiatives that are relatively easy to implement in the first 100 days and that can generate results in 3 to12 months. These no-regret initiatives should close performance gaps in a few critical areas, reduce costs, improve top- and bottom-line performance, and free up cash in order to fuel longer-term initiatives. As new CEOs establish momentum with these initiatives, they should also clearly define the company's goals for improving long-term performance – and how the company will sustain those improvements over time.

A Technology Leader Creates Momentum Through Rapid Moves

At a global technology company, the head of a business unit realized that the organization was not winning the highly competitive war for talent. The company had dropped in the ratings at websites such as Glassdoor.com and in *Fortune* magazine's annual "Best Companies to Work For" review. The results of employee engagement surveys had been falling for years and the unit head knew from personal interactions with employees that they were not happy or motivated to go above and beyond. He wanted a transformation that would increase employee engagement, restore internal pride, and persuade employees to go the extra mile.

But his challenges did not stop there. Customer feedback was very troubling. For example, one customer commented: "When we look at your products, we can see how your organization is structured. Your products are siloed, with incompatible components and broken interfaces – which is just like your siloed organization. We need integrated solutions with components that work together to solve our problems, and we need them now." Such feedback gave the unit head a second impetus for a transformation.

In response, he defined a bold ambition to transform the unit in order to win the war for talent, energize his engineers, deliver the integrated solutions that customers were demanding, and free up resources to deploy on opportunities for growth.

His first step was to conduct a thorough analysis of the root causes of the performance issues. On the basis of this analysis, the unit head defined the ambition for a step-change transformation across multiple dimensions, including growth, innovation, leadership capabilities, workforce quality, organizational efficiency, employee productivity, and culture.

Within the first few weeks, he selected the leadership team to drive the transformation program and communicated the case for change, initially among the top 150 leaders, and then across the business unit.

In the first 100 days, the unit head launched the full transformation program with multiple teams, a program management office, change-management processes, and an employee communications plan. Over the next year, the transformation delivered significant improvements across multiple performance dimensions – the result of a business unit leader conducting a thorough diagnostic evaluation and defining a bold transformation ambition.

The First Weeks: Energize the Organization

In the second step – the initial weeks of a new CEO's tenure – communication becomes critical. Leadership transitions and transformations can be stressful periods for a company, and undergoing both simultaneously can make them doubly so. Yet success requires large numbers of people to go above and beyond to accelerate the pace of change. As a result, new CEOs must carve out the time to energize the organization and build momentum for the collective transformation ambition.

Specifically, new CEOs should start building a compelling case for change from their first day on the job. Initially, new CEOs should make the case to the board of directors and to the senior management team to achieve consensus so that they all "speak with one voice" regarding the transformation. Then, they need to make the case to the entire organization. The case for change should acknowledge the company's heritage and the hard work of employees, but it should also discuss external factors (such as the customer base, competitors, and capital markets), internal metrics (for example, operational and organizational performance and employee engagement), and the necessary measures the company will soon take in response. The case for change is typically made to internal stakeholders in various venues, such as workshops and town hall meetings, as well as through communication channels that allow the CEO to answer important questions on vision, approach, and tactical next steps.

A Consumer Packaged Goods CEO Revamps the Company's Structure and Product Line

A new CEO took over a global consumer packaged goods (CPG) company that had been languishing due to declining sales and a sagging stock price. Recognizing that the company's historic profit core was shrinking and that dramatic action was required, the CEO established a bold vision to change the shape and direction of the entire organization.

Specifically, the CEO split the company in two, creating a slower-growth domestic organization and a rapidly expanding international player. In addition, the least desirable divisions were sold off, which represented approximately 20% of the total portfolio. Finally, the CEO made several acquisitions, particularly in growth areas that could piggyback on the company's existing distribution channels.

Executing this transformation required strong leadership, not only from the CEO but also from the entire senior-management team. Senior leaders were assigned to new organizations on the basis of their skills and experience in various markets. In addition, the new CEO changed the board to include members with a more activist investor mind-set who would help shape the company's growth agenda.

Collectively, these measures more than doubled the company's market value and moved its total shareholder return into the top quartile of the CPG sector.

In addition, leaders should tailor the message and the communication style to the company's situation. Some companies have well-established ideas about their overall direction and sense of purpose; these companies can focus primarily on short-term performance and delay setting a more visionary agenda. Other companies are tired of short-term thinking and constant cuts and need a more compelling story about where the new CEO intends to lead the company. In all cases, it is critical for the CEO to speak with authenticity and a sense of urgency.

A Pharmaceutical Company Transforms Itself and Generates $20 Billion in Value

A global pharmaceutical company had been extremely successful – consistently growing earnings by 15% a year and reinvesting all remaining excess capital. However, management challenged itself to improve performance through a comprehensive transformation of the company. The investor community also indicated that the company could create more value by accelerating earnings growth. As the company began to consider a transformation, it faced an additional challenge – a hostile take-over attempt.

In response, the company launched an extremely rapid initiative to cut activities that generated a low return on investment and restructured to quickly increase earnings. The project team analyzed and redesigned the entire company in only three months and then implemented the new design. Despite the rapid launch, virtually all functions and business units were included in the scope. Notably, the company implemented the transformation through both senior leaders and managers who were several levels down in the organization hierarchy. This approach led to very specific, pragmatic solutions, and it built momentum for the initiative throughout the company's workforce.

Through this transformation, the company cut its annual costs by more than $500 million and increased its earnings growth rate from 15% to more than 20%. These changes yielded an improvement in company value of approximately $20 billion. The transformation also represented a value-creating alternative to the hostile takeover and enabled management to strike a deal with a different acquirer on more favorable terms.

The First 100 Days: Prepare and Launch the Transformation

The first 100 days of the transformation process are critical in that they set the trajectory for the overall transformation – and indeed for the CEO's tenure. Leaders must put the foundation in place during this time, balancing a long-term vision with day-to-day reality. As the transformation starts to take shape and the case for change becomes clear, the CEO must shift gears from planning the transformation to actually leading it. This means immediately kicking off the rapid, no-regret moves that will deliver impact within 3 to 12 months, creating and enabling initiative teams, setting up the overall governance and change-management program for the transformation, and launching the communications plan.

These no-regret initiatives build momentum for the larger effort, win over internal skeptics who may doubt that change is actually happening, generate credibility for the new leadership team, and often free up capital that can be used to fund subsequent measures. As a result, these initiatives further help energize the organization.

The four primary levers for funding the journey are revenue, organizational simplicity (delayering), capital efficiency, and cost reduction (Figure 10.4). In choosing where to start, many companies understandably opt for the two obvious solutions: cost cutting and organizational simplicity. This approach works, but revenue and capital efficiency can often generate a significant impact as well.

A Manufacturer Lays the Groundwork for an Ambitious Transformation

The US housing industry suffered a steep correction following the 2008 global financial crisis. The CEO of a manufacturing company responded with a number of measures that did not improve its financial performance.

Realizing that stronger measures were called for, the CEO decided to launch a more ambitious transformation program, with the goal of increasing earnings before interest and taxes (EBIT) in one year, independent of market growth or price changes.

To prepare for the transformation, seven teams – four composed of employees from business units and three made up of employees from major function areas – developed a roadmap of initiatives around growth, pricing, cost reductions, and operational productivity improvements. Each initiative specified the target EBIT improvement, required actions, milestones, and resources. The company also enabled the teams to meet these aggressive goals by providing them with new analytical frameworks and problem-solving methodologies and tools.

To ensure the overall program delivered on the EBIT ambition, the company set up a steering committee composed of senior executives and a program management office (PMO) to provide governance and drive the pace of the transformation.

The PMO provided rigorous program management, including the monthly tracking of improvements. The reports highlighted any initiatives that were exceeding or falling short of their targets. This gave management a clear view of overall performance and flagged situations that required interventions.

As a result, the company was able to deliver on the ambitious EBIT target set by the CEO. In addition, the business units adopted a continuous-improvement approach to capture gains after the formal transformation program ended.

Once measures are under way, there is a real risk of prematurely declaring victory and moving on to other priorities, which all but assures that the transformation effort will fail. Instead, it is critical to maintain focus and ensure that initiative teams are on track to achieve results. Assuming that some form of project tracking has been put in place, now is the time to ensure that leaders have full transparency into the progress of each initiative. Regular review sessions, facilitated by the program management office (PMO), should provide sufficient information for leaders to know whether – and how – they need to intervene.

Primary levers	Categories	Common tools	Typical impact
Revenue	Pricing	Revamp pricing model, reduce discounts, and develop new pricing capabilities	Raises revenue by 2 to 8 percent
	Sales force effectiveness	Improves customer targeting and enable the sales team	Increases revenue and profit by 10 to 15 percent
	Marketing	Optimize spending and implement data analytics	Reduces marketing costs by 10 to 20 percent; boosts sales volume by 3 to 8 percent
Organizational simplicity	Delayering	Trim the number of layers and increase the spans of control	Shrinks indirect labor costs by 15 to 30 percent; improves accountability, decision making, and operational agility
Capital efficiency	Net-working-capital improvements	Reduce inventory and handle payables and receivables more efficiently	Decreases working capital by 20 to 40 percent
	Fixed-asset productivity	Sell assets, outsource functions, and increase overall equipment effectiveness	Lower capital expenses by 20 to 30 percent; increases EBITDA by 2 to 8 percent
	Project portfolio optimization	Analyze net present value, prioritize projects, and eliminate failed projects	Improves relative TSR by 20 to 40 percent
Cost reduction	COGS and procurement	Decrease spending on promotions, better manage categories and suppliers, and improve procurement	Cuts COGS by 2 to 3 percent and procurement costs by 5 to 20 percent
	Supply chain	Improve logistics, optimize the network, and streamline the product portfolio	Reduces operating expenses by 10 to 30 percent
	Personnel cost	Increase offshoring or outsourcing and reduce head count	Trims labor costs by 20 to 40 percent
	Nonpersonnel cost	Cut spending on travel, utilities, facilities, IT, and services	Lowers overhead costs by 20 percent

Note: EBITDA= earnings before interest, taxes, depreciation, and amortization; TSR=total shareholder return; COGS=cost of goods sold
Source: BCG analysis

Figure 10.4: The Four Primary Levers to Fund the Transformation Journey.

In particular, CEOs should avoid a number of common pitfalls during this phase, including the following:

- Insufficient accountability among the owners and sponsors of the initiatives
- Failure to have in place clear plans and roadmaps, backed with specific actions and milestones that are linked to financial objectives
- A lack of resources and expertise on initiative teams
- Management incentives that do not support the objectives of the transformation
- Failure to engage stakeholders and overcome institutional resistance

The First 18 Months: Drive the Transformation

As the broader transformation begins to gain momentum and initial fund-the-journey efforts begin to take hold, CEOs must launch broader initiatives to win in the medium term, set the new strategy and operating model, and build sustainable performance.

Winning in the Medium Term

This phase requires delivering on transformation objectives that go beyond the short-term goals of earlier, fund-the-journey efforts. The specific objectives will vary by company, but common to all transformations is the need to establish a fundamentally different competitive position, leading to a medium-term step-change in performance. Winning in the medium term could entail a wide range of initiatives to transform, including driving growth, launching a new business model, revamping commercial processes or operations, building digital capabilities and ventures, and transforming internal support functions, such as R&D, IT, or human resources (HR), among others (Figure 10.5).

Compared with funding-the-journey measures, initiatives to win in the medium term are usually more difficult to conceptualize, as they require breakthrough thinking, usually in areas that are less familiar for the organization. These initiatives are also harder to staff and implement, and they call for managing interdependencies across functions and business units.

Growth	Developing the strategy and the operating model to position the company for stronger growth
New business model	Dramatically shifting the business model, including the markets served and the value proposition for customers
Organization	Improving the effectiveness and efficiency of decision making and work process throughout the organization
Commercial	Reshaping sales and marketing by focusing on new markets and increasing the efficiency and effectiveness of spending
Operational	Boosting a company's profitability and cost position across the manufacturing, supply chain, and service operations
Digital	Digitizing the entire value chain—and the company's competitive DNA—by adopting new technologies and rethinking the business strategy
Global	Repositioning a company in a complex global world to take advantage of proper growth opportunities in emerging and developed nations
Innovation and R&D	Increasing the quality and the number of innovations by improving the effectiveness of R&D
IT	Overhauling the core IT infrastructure to enable faster decision making, powerful analytics, efficient process, and improved operations
Support functions	Revamping vital support functions—such as finance, legal, and human resources—to reduces costs and improve performance

Source: BCG analysis

Figure 10.5: The Wide Range of Transformation Initiatives.

A Global Insurer Implements a Value-Based Transformation

A new CEO took over at a global insurance company that had multiple lines of business. The CEO conducted an outside-in analysis to assess the company's current situation, along with its capabilities, its competitive position both globally and in individual markets, and industry analysts' perceptions.

This process identified some clear challenges. The company's return on capital was low, and its capital position was weak. The company also lacked a rigorous process for allocating capital and had inefficient cost structures and an unfocused portfolio of business units, whose performance varied widely.

Through this analysis, the CEO defined the ambition for a transformation and established explicit financial targets. Once he took over the top job, he built momentum for the effort in a series of meetings with the board of directors and the executive committee.

As part of the transformation, the CEO looked at specific insurance segments and restructured the company into 40 "cells." Each cell represented businesses and markets with similar underlying characteristics (for example, vehicle insurance in the UK, pension insurance in Poland, and corporate insurance for large companies in the US). The CEO then assessed the performance of the individual cells across several dimensions through financial analyses and the evaluation of market prospects.

On the basis of the results, the company grouped its businesses into three clusters: "grow" (the top 25 percent), "turnaround" (the middle 50 percent), and "divest" (the bottom 25 percent).

Within the first 100 days, and backed by the senior management team, the CEO had begun communicating a new 18-month initiative to the entire organization. The transformation would include specific corrective actions to improve the cash flow performance of the turnaround units. In addition, the program would reduce costs throughout the company and strengthen the capital management process, with more integrated planning and a better performance-management cycle.

In all, the effort generated more than $400 million in savings in its first year – a savings that included a reduction of 25% in the head count of senior management. That success stemmed from several factors. First, the company took a strictly fact-based approach to analyzing business performance, in part by eliciting an outside-in assessment from the investor and analyst communities. Second, the CEO ensured that all executive committee members had accountability for specific initiatives. And third, the implementation plan was clear from the start, thanks to strong communication and full buy-in from the management team.

Setting the New Strategy and Operating Model

While driving short-term and medium-term initiatives, companies benefit from stepping back and looking at their overall strategy and operating model. This does not need to be a broad strategy- planning exercise. In fact, we find that a targeted workshop-based approach with the senior leadership team – and the appropriate data and analysis – can lead to a strong outcome and do so in a highly efficient manner that doesn't distract the leadership team from driving the overall transformation. This approach ensures that there is buy-in from the top team and that the strategy leads to immediate operational adjustments.

A Bank's Transformation Boosts Customer Satisfaction and Financial Performance

In the wake of the financial crisis, a large bank was struggling to resume a growth trajectory. It suffered from poor profitability and process inefficiency, compared with its peers. The bank also had severe liquidity issues and high write-downs on loans in both core and distant markets. More fundamentally, it had an unclear value proposition for customers and little organizational focus on performance and collaboration among employees.

In response, the CEO and leadership team launched a three-step transformation aimed at improving customer satisfaction and financial results.

The first step was to reorganize the company around the customer experience rather than around divisions and functions, which was the current, silo-based approach. That process clarified the roles for specific functions, and it rewired processes to foster greater collaboration across departments. At the same time, the company revamped its leadership team, making some new hires and giving some current leaders new roles.

The second step was developing a new strategy – new business leaders were tasked with defining the strategy for their units. Those individual strategies were grouped into one major transformation effort that was owned by the CEO and had three specific objectives: better customer satisfaction, greater efficiency, and a performance-based culture.

In the third step – currently under way – the CEO and leadership team are putting their full focus on executing the new strategy.

Building Sustainable Performance

Many organizations that deliver results during a transformation have a tough time sustaining their hard-won performance improvements. The goal of every CEO should be to achieve success during the first 18 months of the transformation program and then maintain it well beyond that point. This is what separates the most transformative CEOs from the rest of the pack. It is imperative for a CEO to own this phase and closely involve the chief human resources officer and other influential leaders across the company.

There are five important aspects to developing the right people and organization required to support a successful, sustainable transformation:

1. Ensure the commitment and change capabilities of the executive team, including their ability to set the right priorities, mobilize and energize initiative teams, and hold themselves accountable for the results.

2. Deploy change-management tools and processes (such as an activist PMO, roadmaps, and rigor testing) to engage stakeholders and deliver results.[2]
3. Install an HR team that can act as a transformation partner, anticipating talent and leadership needs, rather than as a mere service provider.
4. Build a talent pipeline that can help fill crucial roles, and develop capabilities in areas critical for the transformation, such as go-to-market strategies, pricing, sourcing, lean methods, digitization, innovation, and HR.
5. Simplify the organization and culture to sustain high performance in conjunction with the new strategy. This usually entails eliminating waste and low-value work, trimming bureaucracy, implementing shared services, automating processes, and enabling the organization to continue taking these steps on an ongoing basis.

For most new CEOs, the imperative to change is a given; how CEOs respond to this imperative is not. Those who stand out from the pack quickly define a bold transformation ambition – ideally before taking the reins – and then move forward to energize the organization, prepare the program, and drive the transformation. Through quick and decisive actions – while time, the board, and investors are still on their side – new CEOs can seize the opportunity to lead a transformation and put their company on the right trajectory for success.

---

2 For more on rigor testing, see "The Hard Side of Change Management," *Harvard Business Review*, October 2005. https://hbr.org/2005/10/the-hard-side-of-change-management [accessed 9/5/2020].

Martin Reeves, Knut Haanæs, and Kaelin Goulet
Chapter 11
Turning Around the Successful Company

Today's business environment is characterized by rapid, extensive change and unpredictability. The combined effects of digitization, connectivity, globalization, demographic shifts, and social feedback are shaking the foundations of almost all businesses, making sustained growth more valuable and elusive than ever before. In addition, we see that companies – at a time when adaptivity is so crucial – are often hampered by internal complexity that makes change difficult. To compound matters, the diversity of the business environments – in terms of growth, rate of change, and harshness – that global companies face is expanding in a multispeed world. So it is not surprising that many companies find their strategies and business models increasingly out of step with their environments.

Many companies get caught in a "boiling-frog trap," where they fail to recognize the problems and delay efforts to remedy them, thus necessitating a painful and risky step-change transformation. Our analysis suggests that, prior to embarking on such change efforts, fewer than a quarter of companies have outperformed the market and nearly half are systemic underperformers (Figure 11.1).

And while transformations are increasingly common, we know that about 75% of such efforts fail to restore long-term growth and competitiveness. Logically, that's hardly surprising: jumping is inevitably riskier than walking, especially when the bar is high, while often the company's focus is on healthy quarterly earnings rather than sustained competitiveness, encouraging management to adopt a stance of "if it ain't broke, don't fix it." Waiting until performance is already declining, however, not only increases the magnitude of the required adjustment and the organizational difficulty of realizing it but also puts companies in a reactive position, causing them to miss opportunities for preemption, experience building, leadership, and, ultimately, competitive advantage.

There are understandable reasons why companies fail to preemptively transform themselves in the face of change. A company might, for example, do the following:
- Foster a culture that marginalizes new, dissonant perspectives, causing the company to miss or minimize important change signals
- Lapse into a false sense of security because of solid short-term financial performance
- Believe that past performance is indicative of future results
- Have incentives that discourage deviation from the current path

https://doi.org/10.1515/9783110697834-011

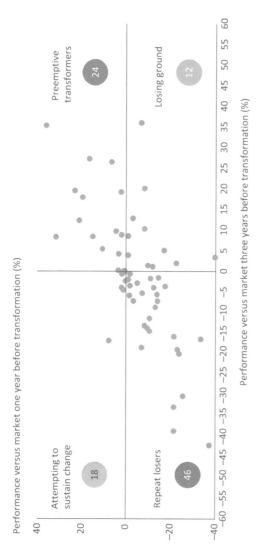

Figure 11.1: Transforming Companies Are Often Playing Catch-Up.

- Focus so closely on short-term performance that the company neglects long-term competitiveness
- Be led by individuals who are stronger at executing within existing models than at building new ones
- Rely too heavily on feedback from currently satisfied customers whose allegiance may shift when a better product comes along
- Wait too long – until evidence of the necessity for change becomes definitive – to act
- Make all the right moves but do so insufficiently, allowing existing power structures to monopolize resources and preventing new ideas from being scaled
- Want to change but find that it is trapped by ongoing structures, processes, and initiatives that are complex and difficult to alter

The fact that it is difficult and uncommon for successful companies to turn themselves around preemptively is, however, no argument against its necessity and possibility. Some companies do, in fact, manage to do so, maintaining performance over a long period of time in the face of external shifts or disruptions and without the need for risky, quantum-leap transformation initiatives. We studied several disruption-prone industries – industrial goods, consumer discretionary goods, IT, health care, telecommunications, and financial services – from 1980 to 2013. And we identified a number of companies that, challenges notwithstanding, managed to generate relatively stable long-term returns. What was their secret sauce?

These businesses possessed several distinct sets of attributes and orientations that drove their preemptive adjustment and resulting impressive performance. We grouped the companies into four categories:

1. *Continuous Adapters*: These companies constantly evolve their business model by making many small changes. McDonald's, for example, successfully rode the baby boom of the 1960s and leveraged the swelling ranks of teenagers and women in the labor force by providing convenience and an inexpensive, selection-rich menu. In the 1970s and 1980s, the company harnessed the globalization megatrend to expand its footprint internationally, successfully deploying its US model in countries around the world.

   Today McDonald's continues to evolve. It adjusts its product portfolio to reflect new trends and consumer preferences – for example, "fast" and "convenient" are now increasingly augmented by "healthy" and "natural." The company also creates new formats, such as cafeterias in Europe and high-end coffee chains in the US, to address competitive threats. It is accelerating the speed with which it adapts to the social contexts of the countries in which it has a presence by franchising to locals. This continuous reshaping has persisted even in the face of internal crises, such as when two CEOs sadly passed away in quick succession in the first few years of the 2000s.

2. *Ambidextrous Players:* A company in this category maintains a balance between exploitation of existing strengths and exploration, even after it has found a successful model. Family succession in public companies is rare; for it to succeed is rarer still, but digital-technology and chip company Qualcomm, led by Paul Jacobs, son of founder Irwin Jacobs, has steadily performed despite massive shifts in telecommunications standards and technologies.

Qualcomm consistently achieves its mission – "to continue to deliver the world's most innovative wireless solutions" – through a business model that uses returns from past successes (including wins in WCDMA, CDMA, and 3G chips) to fuel future ones (such as in LTE).[1] Though most of Qualcomm's revenue comes from chip sales, its mobile-technology licenses provide the company with steady and consistent cash flow that allows it to fund breakthrough R&D and invest in strategic partnerships through Qualcomm Ventures, the company's venture-capital business unit. Qualcomm reaps benefits from both scale and the drive to continuously search for and build the next big thing in wireless.

3. *Industry Shakers:* These companies seek to drive industry-level change rather than become victims of it. A headline in *The New York Times* on October 21, 2013, boomed "Sales Are Colossal, Shares Are Soaring. All Amazon Is Missing Is a Profit."[2] Yet because CEO Jeff Bezos so actively commits to a long-term view and has repeatedly delivered disruptive innovation, investors treat Amazon like a blue-chip stock. Indeed, Amazon continually generates razor-thin profits precisely because it continually reinvests in its future – in refrigerated warehouses for groceries, in same-day delivery in urban centers, and in data servers and analytics, for example.

Bezos founded Amazon in 1994 with a vision that e-commerce would fundamentally disrupt retailing. He chose books as his initial product focus because demand was large, prices were relatively low, and the range of selection was enormous – a combination he deemed ideally suited to the online channel. His foray was so disruptive to the book-selling industry that many

1 WCDMA = Wideband Code Division Multiple Access; CDMA = Code Division Multiple Access; LTE = Long-Term Evolution.

2 David Streitfeld, "Sales Are Colossal, Shares Are Soaring. All Amazon Is Missing Is a Profit," *The New York Times*, October 21, 2013. https://www.nytimes.com/2013/10/22/technology/sales-are-colossal-shares-are-soaring-all-amazoncom-is-missing-is-a-profit.html [accessed 9/5/2020].

brick-and-mortar retailers ultimately capitulated and chose to sell their wares through Amazon's online storefront, allowing the company to leverage its first-mover advantages in supply chain innovation, product selection, and the setting of platform standards. But Amazon did not rest on its laurels. It self-disrupted its book business with the launch of its e-reader, the Kindle, in 2007; by 2011, the company was selling more e-books than print copies.

What's next? Amazon continues to succeed by combining its ability to recognize and position itself optimally to leverage nascent long-term trends with its ability to create and set standards for new markets.

4. *Portfolio Shifters*: A company of this type runs a portfolio of businesses and actively adjusts its emphasis over time. Industrial conglomerate 3M, for example, has more than 35 business units divided among six (through 2012) reporting segments. While the sales contribution by segment has not changed dramatically over time – the company's Industrial and Transportation segment, for example, contributed 34.6% of the company's overall sales in 2012, compared with 27.4% in 2003 – the underlying portfolio companies and products have.

   3M's approach to strategic acquisitions and divestments reflects the evolving demand landscape. The company makes acquisitions in anticipation of future growth trends – such as its purchase of Cogent Systems, a manufacturer of automated fingerprint-identification systems, in 2010 – and it spun off its print film division in 1996 in advance of the rise of digital imaging. This shifting mix, combined with tight financial management, has allowed the firm, remarkably, to increase dividend payouts to shareholders on an annual basis for the past 55 years, and it keeps operating margins well above 20 percent.

Most important, these steady performers have not achieved consistent success by staying the same. Figure 11.2 contrasts these companies' orientations with those of two types of more reactive, and ultimately far less successful, businesses (transformers and dinosaurs). Their distinct approaches to remaining dynamic draw on a common menu of elements:

- *An External Orientation*: They actively strive to pick up change signals from the outside environment and act upon them.
- *A Long-Term Perspective*: They focus on sustainable competitiveness rather than on short-term financial results alone.
- *Ambidexterity*: They have a balanced emphasis on exploitation and exploration.
- *Adaptivity*: They constantly adjust their strategy and organization to changes in the external environment and seek to uncover new possibilities through experimentation.

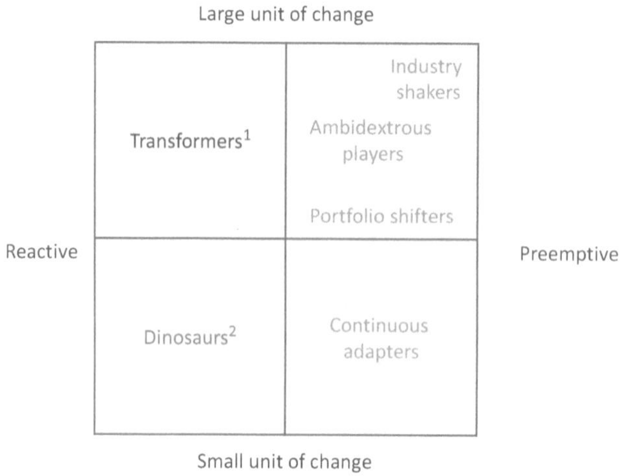

Large unit of change

Transformers[1]	Industry shakers Ambidextrous players Portfolio shifters
Dinosaurs[2]	Continuous adapters

Reactive   Preemptive

Small unit of change

1. Transformers are companies that suffer a decline in performance and then employ a turnaround strategy and business model innovation to recover and flourish 2. Dinosaurs are companies that fail to adapt their business model in response to volatility and change, and thus theirbusiness ultimately decays
Source: BCG analysis

Figure 11.2: Outperformers Fall into Four Categories.

- *A Disruptive Mentality:* They have a drive to disrupt both the external environment and their own business and are prepared to be disrupted themselves.
- *A Healthy Paranoia:* They have a lack of hubris and are constantly aware of their competitive vulnerability, independent of their current financial performance.
- *Resource Fluidity:* They have the ability and willingness to shift resources smoothly across the portfolio and organization, and they do not shy away from promptly exiting eroding but still functioning elements of the business.
- *A Constant Focus on Simplicity*: They avoid buildups of complexity and rigidity.

Leaders of all enterprises today need to look beyond short-term financial performance, watch for potential disruptions and shifts, and then preemptively address them. They need to be prepared to disrupt to avoid finding themselves victims of disruption. They need to address the imperatives of simplicity, adaptivity, and business model innovation. In short, successful companies can only perpetuate their successes through continuous preemptive renewal.

Lars Fæste, Ib Löfgrén, Martin Reeves, and Jens Kengelbach

Chapter 12
How Bold CEOs Succeed at M&A Turnarounds

Growth is difficult, especially in a slowing economy, and sometimes M&A can offer a solution. Although few M&A deals wind up creating value, CEOs with a proven ability to transform an organization and improve performance in difficult conditions can create massive value by picking up a troubled business or brand – often at a discount. It's a bold idea: buying distressed assets, turning them around, and integrating them to produce a company that is much stronger than the sum of its parts.

An analysis of 1,400 M&A-based turnarounds between 2005 and 2018 found that the TSR of winning deals was 25 percentage points higher than that of unsuccessful deals. We identified five factors that can increase the ability of bold CEOs to succeed with such turnarounds:

1. **Willingness to act quickly.** The single biggest factor in a turnaround deal's success is a willingness to take bold and rapid action. Buyers that launched a turnaround in the first year after a deal closed generated 12 percentage points more in TSR than those that waited until later. Engaging quickly generates momentum and frees up capital, both of which can spur longer-term initiatives. Early action also helps boost investors' confidence, which is a key factor in turnaround success. Successful CEOs treat speed as their friend.

2. **Ambitious synergy targets.** Leaders need to aim high, with ambitious synergy targets factoring in both increased revenue and reduced costs. These should be stretch goals that look at the "full potential" of the turnaround: improvements to the acquired company, improvements to the buyer, and synergies from combining the two (Figure 12.1). CEOs who set ambitious targets, announced them externally, and reported on progress generated higher TSR in the years following the close of an acquisition.

3. **Sufficient investment in transformation.** Turnaround programs cost money – to close plants, restructure business units, or repair assets that have become obsolete. Rather than treating these as expenses and dragging the program out over a long period of time, successful leadership teams treat them as investments (often as restructuring charges), and companies that invested more and moved faster than the average for their industry performed better over time.

https://doi.org/10.1515/9783110697834-012

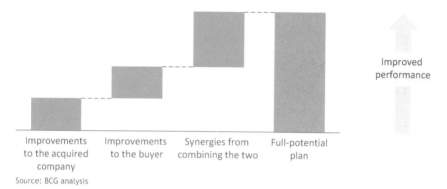

Improvements to the acquired company   Improvements to the buyer   Synergies from combining the two   Full-potential plan

Improved performance

Source: BCG analysis

Figure 12.1: A "Full Potential" Turnaround Plan.

4. **A long-term orientation**. CEOs who are integrating a troubled business need to consider the short term and make tactical and operational moves that will generate the necessary funding. But those who can balance this short-term perspective with a long-term strategic orientation show better financial returns over time. These leaders do not get so caught up in daily crises that they miss emerging opportunities. They invest more in digital and R&D and less in capital improvements, and their long-term orientation allows them to improve their strategic positioning.

5. **A well-defined purpose**. A growing body of BCG research shows that companies with goals and aspirations that go beyond profits perform better over time.[1] The same principle applies to M&A turnarounds. Acquiring companies that spell out a common purpose can motivate and align employees around long-term goals. Leadership teams and employees will push themselves hard on a turnaround program if they see the long-term objective.

While each of these five factors on its own can improve the results of an M&A turnaround, a combination of two or more is even more powerful. In fact, there is a direct correlation between the number of factors that a company takes into account and the boost in three-year TSR from the deal.

---

1 Cathy Carlisi, Jim Hemerling, Julie Kilmann, Dolly Meese, and Doug Shipman, "Purpose with the Power to Transform Your Organization," *BCG Publications*, May 15, 2017. https://www.bcg.com/publications/2017/transformation-behavior-culture-purpose-power-transform-organization [accessed 9/5/2020].

The following three case studies show what successful M&A turnarounds look like in practice.

Automotive: Groupe PSA

Automaker Opel had long underperformed its peers, losing about $1.1 billion annually starting in 1999. In 2017, the company was bought by Groupe PSA, the parent company of Peugeot, Citroën, Vauxhall Motors, and DS Automobiles. Groupe PSA had launched a highly successful turnaround program of its own in 2014, leading to a strong rebound in profitability and market capitalization. Now it wanted to build on that momentum and the operational and strategic improvements it had made by turning around newly acquired Opel.

The deal closed in August 2017, and Groupe PSA immediately began making changes. It thinned the ranks of upper management at Opel by about 25%. It also reached a deal with labor unions to eliminate 3,700 jobs through buyouts and reduce the standard workweek from 40 hours to 35, leading to a significant drop in labor costs. Finally, it reduced fixed costs by 27% in marketing and other areas.

The turnaround also focused on streamlining production, which was unnecessarily complex because of a large number of models and options. For instance, one basic hatchback model had 57 infotainment systems for customers to choose from. To simplify, Opel reduced the number of car platforms – the basic chassis – from nine to just two. It also scaled back the number of engine groups from ten to four. And those 57 infotainment options were cut back to a reasonable ten.

Turnarounds in asset-heavy industries like automotive typically take years to generate results, but the program at Opel began doing so almost immediately. The company lost roughly $200 million in the second half of 2017, a period that included its first five months under Groupe PSA's ownership. But by the first half of 2018, it had already returned to black ink, posting positive earnings of $583 million. In 2018 overall, it earned $960 million – the highest revenues in the company's 157-year history. Opel now has profit margins of about 5%, on par with those of Volkswagen.

Groupe PSA's acquisition and transformation of Opel – coming on the heels of its own earlier transformation – have refurbished a storied brand and helped the company regain its position as one of the top-performing automakers in the world.

Biopharmaceuticals: Sanofi

In 2009, French pharmaceutical company Sanofi was in acquisition mode. Many of its products were losing patent protection, and the company wanted to shift from traditional drugs into biologics. One potential target was Genzyme.

From 2000 through 2010, Genzyme had grown rapidly, but manufacturing issues at two of its facilities had halted production and led to a shortage of key drugs in its portfolio. Sales plunged, the US Food and Drug Administration issued fines, and investors called for management changes. But many features of the company still met Sanofi's needs, including a lucrative orphan drug business with no patent cliff and a strong history of innovation. Sanofi made an offer: $20 billion or $74 per share, which was roughly Genzyme's value before the manufacturing problems hit.

Management laid out a bold ambition and moved fast. The company streamlined manufacturing, opening a new plant to reduce the drug shortage, and simplified operations to remove bottlenecks at existing plants. Next, it moved sales and marketing for some of Genzyme's businesses, including oncology, biosurgery, and renal products, under the Sanofi brand. It also reduced the overall sales force by about 2,000 people.

Genzyme's R&D pipeline was integrated into Sanofi, and a new portfolio review process led to the cessation of some studies and the reprioritization of others. About 30% of Genzyme's cost base was reduced through the integration with Sanofi. Genzyme's diagnostics unit was sold off, and about 8,000 full-time employees were eliminated in the EU and North America.

The moves generated positive results fast. Overall, the integration led to about $700 million in cost reductions through synergies. By 2011, the company was back in expansion mode with 5% revenue growth, increasing to 17% in 2012. Only about 13% of Sanofi's revenue came from Genzyme products, but these were poised for strong growth, positioning Sanofi as a global leader in rare-disease therapeutics and spurring its evolution into a dominant player in biologics.

Industrial Equipment: Konecranes

Konecranes is a global provider of industrial and port cranes equipment and services. Several years ago, in the face of increased competition, Konecranes was struggling to cut costs or grow organically. In 2016, it bought a business unit from Terex Corporation called Material Handling & Port Solutions (MHPS), its principal competitor. The MHPS business included several brands that complemented Konecranes' products and services, along with some sizable overlaps in technology and manufacturing networks.

Before the deal closed, Konecranes drafted an ambitious full-potential plan to generate about $160 million in synergies within three years through cost reductions and new business. That represented a 70% improvement over the joint company's pro forma financials. The turnaround plan encompassed all main businesses and functions across both legacy Konecranes and MHPS operations and included the following measures:
- Reducing procurement spending through increased volumes
- Consolidating service locations
- Aligning technological standards and platforms
- Closing some manufacturing sites
- Streamlining corporate functions
- Adopting more efficient processes
- Optimizing the go-to-market approach
- Identifying new avenues of growth

The full program consisted of 350 individual initiatives organized into nine major work streams and aligned with the overall organization structure to create clear accountabilities and tie the program's impact directly to financial results. Still, many of the initiatives were complex by nature, so solid planning and rigorous program management and reporting have been critical.

Konecranes also carried out a holistic baseline survey to assess the cultures of the two organizations and define a joint target culture. An extensive cultural development and communications plan featured strongly in the early days of the integration.

The company has reported on its progress to investors as part of its quarterly earnings calls, and two years into the three-year plan, it has hit or exceeded its targets. That performance has earned praise from investors, leading to a share price increase of more than 50% since the acquisition was announced.

Turnarounds are tough, and those involving M&A are even harder. Yet there is also significant value to be had, provided CEOs understand the factors leading to success. As growth slows in many industries – and in the overall economy – companies that take these factors into account can give themselves the best odds of success. At a time when other companies hunker down, they will be able to spot opportunities and pounce on them.

Part III: **The Next Level of Managing Change**

Jim Hemerling, Diana Dosik, and Shaheer Rizvi

Chapter 13
A Leader's Guide to Always-On Transformation

For leaders in large corporations, business today often feels like being on a steep treadmill with the speed control set to max. Three months ago, the company may have finished a cost-reduction transformation to remove management layers and streamline operations. Before it is even clear that the changes have taken root, a disruption in Asia requires implementing a new go-to-market model for several countries. And right around the corner is another large-scale transformation effort, using new digital technology to improve the delivery of services and tap new revenue streams.

Welcome to the era of "always-on" transformation. Across virtually all industries, unprecedented disruption and market turbulence – due to globalization, technological innovation, changing regulations, and other factors – are challenging established business models and practices, and requiring organizations to launch more frequent transformations in response. To keep up, companies need to undertake many different types of transformation (Figure 13.1). Any one of these, or several, can be under way at a company at any given time. BCG's research shows that 85% of companies that have undertaken transformations over the past decade have pursued more than one type, with the most common being organizational, operational, and rapid financial improvements.

We define a transformation as a profound change in a company's strategy, business model, organization, culture, people, or processes – either enterprise-wide or within a specific business unit, function, or market. A transformation is not an incremental shift in some aspect of the business but a fundamental change aimed at achieving a sustainable, quantum improvement in performance and, ultimately, shareholder value.[1] Unlike continuous improvement – which focuses on small-scale changes that start with employees and percolate up through the organization – always-on transformation requires a series of much larger, interdependent initiatives that are driven by top management.

---

[1] For an explanation of BCG's transformation framework, see "Transformation: The Imperative to Change," *BCG report*, November 2014. https://www.bcg.com/publications/2014/people-organization-transformation-imperative-change [accessed 9/5/2020].

https://doi.org/10.1515/9783110697834-013

	Type	Description
Enterprise wide or business unit-based transformation	Turnaround	Making the short-term moves necessary to save a company that is struggling or even failing (for example, facing a pending liquidity crisis)
	Rapid financial boost	Boosting the bottom line rapidly, through measure such as reducing costs, increasing revenue, simplifying the organization, or improving capital efficiency
	Growth	Developing the strategy and operating model to position the company for stronger growth
	Business model	Dramatically shifting the business model, including the markets served and the value proposition for customers
	Digital	Digitizing the entire value chain–and the company's competitive DNA–by adopting new technologies and rethinking the business strategy
	Global	Repositioning a company to take advantage of growth opportunities in emerging and developed markets
	Organization	Improving the efficiency and effectiveness of decision making and work process throughout the organization
Function specific transformation	Innovation and R&D	Increasing the quality and quantity of innovation through more effective R&D
	Commercial	Reshaping sales and marketing function by focusing on new markets and increasing the efficiency and effectiveness of spending
	Operational	Boosting a company's profitability and production across the manufacturing supply chain and services operations
	IT	Overhauling the core IT infrastructure to enable faster decision making, powerful analytics, efficient processes, and improved operations
	Support functions	Revamping vital support functions–such as finance, legal, and human resources–to reduce costs and improve performance

Source: BCG analysis

Figure 13.1: Companies Require Different Types of Transformation.

In this new era, the ability to implement transformation has become a competitive differentiator. Yet most companies are not reaping rewards from transformation efforts. According to our analysis, only 24% of companies that complete transformations outperform competitors in their industries in both the short and long term.

Whether the objective is rapid bottom-line improvements or more fundamental changes to business and operating models, company leaders need a more effective approach. Rather than focusing on short-term targets alone (for example, a 20% improvement in operating efficiency), companies need to go much deeper in order to sustainably improve performance through individual transformations and to ingrain the ability to transform to meet future needs.

In this chapter, we discuss the main reasons that the current approach to transformation falls short, and we describe specific changes that organizations can make to achieve better results. Specifically, we discuss six organizational imperatives that companies need to focus on – along with new roles for HR and leadership – in order to thrive in the era of always-on transformation.

Root Causes of Failure

Why do most companies fail to meet their transformation goals? There are several reasons. The first is that companies typically adopt a short-term, top-down approach to implementation. Transformations are energy intensive and are often executed under tremendous pressure from boards and other stakeholders – frequently as a reaction to flagging performance – which leads management teams to seek fast fixes and immediate results. Consequently, many companies simply seek to compel employees to change their behaviors. They motivate through carrots and sticks – mostly sticks – rather than tapping into the intrinsic motivators that can spur employees to improve performance in a sustainable manner.

Second, successful transformations increasingly require changes to business and operating models, which in turn require new ways of thinking and working. Yet more often than not, companies fail to build the capabilities required to enable people to work in new and different ways. Without adequate attention to enabling new behaviors and ways of working, companies do not achieve and sustain the results they desire.

A third reason underlying the failure to reach transformation goals is that many companies approach transformation in a one-off manner – treating each initiative as an independent event. Under this flawed thinking, they essentially put up scaffolding around one aspect of the organization, focus intently on changing some part of it, and then take down the scaffolding, thinking that they can revert to steady-state operations.

This kind of short-term, one-off approach is akin to the way some schools prepare students for standardized tests. In an attempt to improve test scores, teachers try to cram knowledge into students' heads – basically "teaching to the test" for a few frenzied weeks leading up to the tests. That approach can work – scores often do go up to meet the short-term objective of doing well on the tests – but it doesn't meet the fundamental goals of education: making sure students learn the underlying skills that will help them succeed over the long term.

Six Key Imperatives

Companies that are not just surviving but thriving in the era of always-on transformation focus on six specific imperatives (Figure 13.2). We identified these six by reflecting on the many transformations that BCG has been involved with over the past decade – particularly multiple transformations within the same company. All six have one unifying trait: they are aimed at putting people first.

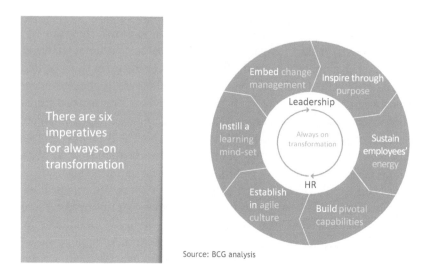

Source: BCG analysis

Figure 13.2: Six Key Imperatives for Always-On Transformation.

Management teams that focus on these six imperatives can create a new type of organization in which transformation is not a temporary, bolted-on approach to delivering one-off, short-term results but rather an ongoing and integral means of delivering superior performance. Although we have observed some companies that have successfully integrated some of these elements, very few have incorporated all six. Those companies that do so are positioning themselves to thrive in the era of always-on transformation.

Inspire Through Purpose

Most transformations focus on financial or operational goals (for example, increasing revenue or improving operating efficiency). While such goals are extremely important – and motivating to the board, investors, and senior management – they tend to be an underwhelming motivator for the majority of employees.

In order to get employees to buy into a transformation, its goals must be tied to the deeper and more inspiring purpose of the company (which transcends any given transformation). BrightHouse, an independent division of BCG that helps companies embrace a more purpose-driven culture, has found that when organizations can clearly define and communicate their purpose to employees – that is, the "why" – these employees feel that they are part of something bigger. And when employees believe in the company's purpose, they are intrinsically motivated to go above and beyond their day-to-day duties.

A Retailer Uses Purpose to Inspire Employees and Improve Business Results

A North American retailer had a successful history of increasing sales through aggressive pricing and maintaining margins by keeping costs low. However, it faced increasing pressure from competitors, and it was struggling to motivate retail sales associates and engage with customers in a meaningful way. In response, it launched a transformation with a strong emphasis on purpose.

The company's leaders conducted deep qualitative and quantitative research to determine the most salient ways to connect with customers and in-store associates on a more emotional level. They also explored the company's corporate history and organizational strengths in order to understand its values and heritage. As a result of this process, the management team defined a new purpose and launched a comprehensive transformation of its stores – with that purpose as its foundation – aimed at improving everything from customer interactions to merchandising. It tested the new approach in 20 pilot stores and then in a full division. Based on compelling test results, the company has begun rolling out the new approach to the rest of its locations.

With this purpose as a guiding principle, the transformation has been highly successful. Customer-experience and associate-engagement scores have improved significantly, as have key financial metrics such as same-store sales and market share.

Once a company has formulated and articulated its clear overarching purpose, all subsequent transformations should link directly to it. Moreover, all employees should be able to see how their contributions help the company succeed in those transformations – and better fulfill the company's broader purpose. All three elements are crucial: a well-defined and shared purpose for the company, a specific link to the transformation at hand, and a clear connection between employees' actions and contributions to the company's objectives.

Some practical actions that companies can take to embed a clear purpose in their transformation efforts include the following:

- Ensuring that the company has a clearly defined and articulated purpose that captures the "why" underlying how it functions
- Translating the transformation's purpose into language and objectives that hold meaning for individual employees (beyond making money for shareholders)
- Communicating the company's objectives consistently throughout the transformation effort – starting with senior management down through peer-level employees
- Using creative methods – such as inspiring videos and staff events – to engage employees so that they clearly understand the purpose of the transformation and how they can contribute to it

Sustain Employees' Energy

In an environment of always-on transformation, companies need to treat transformation as if it were a triathlon, not a sprint. Transformations are typically intense efforts that require employees to go beyond their normal baseline workload. An all-out sprint may work for the first few months, but eventually fatigue will set in and employees will be less able to contribute – particularly when another transformation is likely right around the corner.

A better way is to think like triathletes, who have to swim, bike, and run. Triathletes learn to pace themselves so that they can excel in all three disciplines. Rather than asking employees to maintain a high level of engagement nonstop, companies need to intersperse commitments to high-demand transformation projects with time for true recovery. With the right pacing, employees will be able to engage enthusiastically on each new assignment asked of them, without losing energy. (Notably, there is one group that simply cannot take a break: the senior leadership team.)

Among the practical actions companies can take to sustain the energy of their workforce are the following:

- Recruiting employees who thrive in a transformation environment
- Addressing resistance openly and overcoming resistance through candid conversations
- Structuring initiatives and employees' roles to contribute to personal growth and development
- Allowing employees to recover from energy-intensive transformation efforts before assigning them to the next one

Build Pivotal Capabilities

Companies are increasingly embarking on transformations that rewire the way they operate – including new business models, digitization, and fundamental changes to the roles of business units and functions. As a result, companies invariably need to build new capabilities, such as processes, knowledge, skills, tools, and behaviors. Knowing how to identify and develop these capabilities in any given transformation is pivotal to success.

A Software Company Builds New Capabilities as Part of a Transformation

A leading software and services company recently launched a transformation to change its business model from on-premises licensed software to cloud-hosted software as a service (SaaS). Transforming the company to support the new business model necessitated changes to the organization's design, culture, and leadership. The transformation also required building new capabilities that are essential to succeeding with SaaS.

For example, under the old model, the company responded to customer problems in a highly reactive manner because it had no way of knowing that customers were experiencing issues until they reported them. However, as part of the SaaS approach, the company rolled out real-time usage dashboards that allowed it to be proactive in anticipating problems. The dashboards helped the company to spot usage patterns, predict customer needs, and address them rapidly – which it bundles into a new capability known as "customer success." The company has also committed to creating new processes and developing new skills required to deliver against these metrics.

Integrating this new capability has also required rethinking the organization design – considering where best to place the new capability – along with changes to the company's culture in order to improve its performance over time. For example, by giving the customer success capability a higher profile within the organization, the company was able to attract higher-skilled employees and give them greater say in how the SaaS model functions for specific clients.

A company seeking to become better at innovation may need additional capabilities in primary research, product development, assessing the market potential of new ideas, building a business case, and getting new products to market quickly. To build these capabilities, the company will need to improve its understanding of changes in customer behavior. It may need to develop skills in rapid prototyping and design-to-value methodologies. At the employee level, required changes could well include revamping recruiting strategies and approaches to training, coaching, and development, along with redefining roles and upgrading performance management.

Companies can take the following practical actions to build pivotal capabilities:

- Assessing which capabilities are critical to the success of the transformation by talking to experts and analyzing competitors
- Understanding the root causes of capability gaps – including behavioral and technical issues
- Developing plans to close capability gaps and committing the necessary resources – usually requiring a combination of changes to processes, upgraded skills, new tools, and actions to reinforce new ways of working
- Deciding when to build these capabilities organically and when to accelerate the process through acquisitions, partnerships, or outsourcing

Establish an Agile Culture

In a business landscape characterized by constant and broad-ranging disruption, the ability to rapidly change course in response to market shifts and to enable employees to adapt the way they work becomes critical. Truly agile organizations don't just accommodate change and mandate speed – they ingrain these elements into the company's culture and ways of working.

A Manufacturer Creates a Playbook for Responding to Market Corrections

Facing a downturn in demand during the 2008 recession, a large North American manufacturer undertook a major transformation in order to reduce costs. The company's situation was dire; sales volume had fallen by more than 50 percent, even as prices dropped sharply. The initial transformation was successful – delivering $2 billion in value over three years with a significant jump in market share – yet management realized that was only the first step. The company would need to be agile enough to respond to similar market disruptions in the future.

To meet this need, the manufacturer created a cost-cutting playbook with three tiers for different situations (normal economy, slight downturn, and severe downturn). In a normal economy, the playbook specifies the baseline level of fixed costs. In the event of a slight downturn or a severe downturn, the playbook specifies which costs should be cut first. For example, in a severe downturn in which demand falls dramatically, it makes little sense to spend on selling or marketing at trade shows, so those costs get cut.

With the playbook, business leaders know where their line of business stands in the company's order of priorities, so they are less likely to try "protecting their turf" by obstructing crucial cost reductions. This awareness increases the company's responsiveness and agility by removing long deliberations and politics from the cost-cutting process. In addition, the playbook is flexible in that the company can adjust its priorities for the different tiers should there be long-term shifts in the market.

Agile companies are not burdened by excessive layers of management or bureaucracy. Employees have a wide degree of autonomy and are trusted to resolve many of the issues they face without direct oversight. They are able to take on new roles and responsibilities and to swiftly adapt to new ways of working. They are quick to acquire knowledge of new topics, with the understanding that another change is almost certainly coming soon. In addition, agile companies encourage experimentation, and they don't fear uncertainty. Managers at these companies celebrate and reward risk taking, and they don't punish failure (only the failure to experiment).

Companies can build agility by making some of the following changes, which we have observed in practice helping companies implement transformations:

- Stripping out bureaucracy – removing organizational layers, simplifying rules and policies, and identifying and eliminating noncritical work
- Hiring people and empowering employees who are excited by dynamic workplaces and taking steps to foster this attitude in other employees
- Publicly celebrating employees who successfully adapt to new roles and behaviors
- Developing mobility programs to help employees gain experience in different roles and learn new ways of thinking, so that they understand how various departments function and what they require to succeed

Instill a Learning Mindset

Companies that wish to lay the groundwork for future transformations need to foster a learning mindset across the entire organization. Such an organizational mindset entails spurring people to seek out new knowledge, experiment with it, share it, and ultimately use it to improve the company's performance. For that reason, employees at organizations with a learning mindset are encouraged to follow their curiosity and challenge conventional thinking. They develop creative ways to improve processes and find better ways to do things. This kind of learning culture requires a free exchange of ideas, an acknowledgment that many new ideas will fail, and an understanding that such failures are an inevitable part of progress.

A Technology Company Focuses on Learning across the Entire Organization

A large technology company has firmly embedded "learning" throughout its entire organization. State-of-the-art knowledge-management software helps the company share ideas and give real-time feedback on projects. The company also invests heavily in individual learning, through an internal library of courses and tuition reimbursement for college-level programs. The organization's strong HR-analytics function helps managers make smarter hires and better align talent with the company's strategic goals. For example, the company captures interview data during the hiring process and uses profiles of employees to determine which characteristics lead to success. The company also studied the factors behind female attrition and revamped its benefits package for new mothers. When it realized that the top-performing employees delivered significantly greater value than employees who perform in the middle range, the company revamped its compensation structure to provide larger rewards for top performers.

Transformations can be ideal environments in which to promote learning because they demand creative problem solving and new ideas. To encourage the behaviors associated with learning, companies can take the following actions:

- Establishing a central knowledge-management function that codifies learning and creates networks of experts on specific topics
- Encouraging employees to approach problems in unconventional ways
- Getting business units and functions to collaborate and share knowledge across organizational borders
- Celebrating creative and innovative teams
- Setting up regular meetings in which employees from multiple teams, business units, and functions share ideas and experiences

Embed Change Management

As mentioned earlier, one of the key challenges in transformation is that companies tend to see each initiative as a temporary, one-off event. As a result, companies consider change management as part of the temporary scaffolding of a given transformation effort. Instead, companies need to build change-management skills, make tools available across the broader organization, and consider change management to be a core competency among the extended leadership team.[2]

Rather than rolling out each new transformation initiative from scratch – and moving temporary scaffolding around the organization for each one – companies should consider setting up an internal transformation office to embed change management in the organization. Companies with a permanent transformation office have dedicated resources to, and institutional expertise in, all aspects of change management, which they can deploy as needed. Properly structured, a transformation office can provide oversight over all transformation efforts, help prioritize and sequence transformations, design individual transformation initiatives, and track progress. The transformation office can also serve as a repository of change-management capabilities in the company. Some companies have also found it helpful to include related activities – such as lean initiatives and continuous improvement – under the overall mandate of the transformation office in order to ensure the coordination and alignment of all performance-improvement programs.

Some practical actions companies can take to ingrain change management include the following:

- Making transformation-focused positions attractive to employees – for example, by creating a competitive application process and emphasizing the opportunity to develop relationships with top management
- Establishing strong change-management processes that help transformation leaders plan and roll out change initiatives – including building a case for change, securing stakeholder engagement, designing roadmaps, and implementing rigor testing
- Learning by doing – making the development of internal change-management capabilities an important part of each change initiative

HR as a Strategic Transformation Partner

All of the above imperatives have enormous implications for a company's people practices and HR policies. As such, HR must play a larger role in this always-on transformation era. Ultimately, HR needs to participate actively in senior leadership discussions, help develop the company's strategy and transformation agenda,

---

2 See "Changing Change Management: A Blueprint That Takes Hold," *BCG report*, December 2012. https://www.bcg.com/publications/2012/change-management-postmerger-integration-changing-change-management [accessed 9/5/2020].

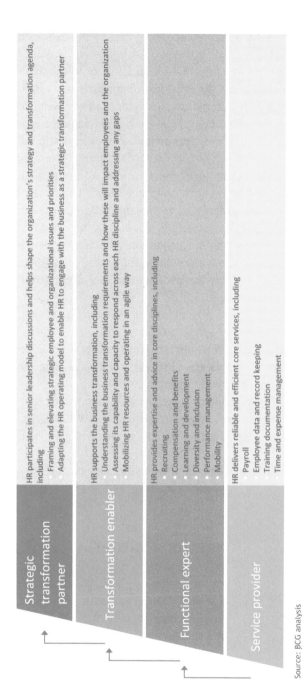

Figure 13.3: HR Must Evolve Into a Strategic Transformation Partner.

and support the alignment of specific functions with the company's priorities. To embrace this role, HR needs to evolve beyond its traditional supporting function to become a true strategic transformation partner (Figure 13.3). Equally important, the company's senior leadership needs to support HR's expanded role.

Specifically, HR must understand the requirements of the transformation and how they impact the company's employee-related processes and HR disciplines. It must work with company leaders to understand how employees and the organization will enable the company's strategy. It must anticipate the implications of every change initiative on employees and the organization. It must know whether the company has the capability and the capacity to meet its strategic goals. All the while, HR must keep pace with the organization and operate with agility as transformations unfold.

As Figure 13.3 shows, HR's expanded role requires a new set of capabilities. For example, frequent product and strategy shifts will call for regular upgrades to the organization structure. HR should work with line-of-business leaders to decide how the organization needs to adapt and then orchestrate the process – with the expectation that the organization design will soon need to be upgraded again. Similarly, in a more volatile environment, strategic workforce planning becomes more important – and more difficult. HR must take the lead in assessing and anticipating emerging skills gaps and in developing strategies to meet future needs for talent.[3]

Implications for Leadership

There are many things that company leaders must do in any transformation, including defining the ambition; energizing the organization; and preparing, launching, and driving the transformation.[4] In the era of always-on transformation, there are two additional critical success factors for leaders: applying a leadership approach that is both directive and inclusive, and charting the optimal path for ingraining the six imperatives described above.

---

3 See "Transforming Technology Companies: Putting People First," *BCG article*, November 2014. https://www.bcg.com/publications/2014/transforming-technology-companies-putting-people-first [accessed 9/5/2020].

4 For more on how incoming leaders at organizations should handle transformation, see "The New CEO's Guide to Transformation: Turning Ambition into Sustainable Results," *BCG Focus*, May 2015. https://www.bcg.com/publications/2015/transformation-change-management-new-ceo-guide-transformation [accessed 9/5/2020].

1. **Apply directive *and* inclusive leadership.** As noted earlier, one of the
inherent challenges of transformations is that they often take place under intense pressure to achieve rapid results. Under these conditions, leaders cannot afford to be hands-off after they set a broad vision; they cannot delegate
the execution and stand back to wait for results. To deliver a fundamental
change in performance at an accelerated pace, leaders not only need to define
and articulate the vision but also must clearly articulate strategic priorities,
set the transformation ambition and milestones, and hold employees accountable for results through regular checkpoints. Still, while strong directive leadership is necessary, in the era of always-on transformation it is not
sufficient – because it fails to provide the motivation required for sustained
performance and the new ways of thinking needed to develop fundamentally
better ways of working. Instead, leaders need to develop a more balanced,
"transformational leadership" approach that is both directive and inclusive
(Figure 13.4).

Source: BCG analysis

Figure 13.4: Transformational Leadership Must Be Directive and Inclusive.

Inclusive leaders involve employees early in the process – well before implementation – and make clear how their contributions help fulfill the larger purpose and objectives of the transformation. By taking these steps, the company's
leadership is able to secure a more authentic commitment from employees.
Inclusive leaders also mobilize and empower teams by giving them some

freedom, within a prescribed framework, to define and implement specific initiatives in the transformation. And they solicit honest feedback and take it into account in modifying the transformation in light of issues that have come up during implementation.

Transformational leadership that is both directive and inclusive clearly raises the bar for executives. It requires an investment in time, energy, and management focus when demands on leaders are, typically, already very high. The bandwidth required to lead in this way is often one of the biggest constraints in a transformation. However, in our experience, making the needed investment of time, energy, and management focus pays off through more efficient and effective execution and more sustainable results. Over time, as the transformation takes hold, leaders can shift to a more delegating style.

A Global Consumer Company Prepares for the Era of Always-on Transformation

For more than a decade, a leading global consumer company has delivered double-digit revenue growth and strong profitability. To achieve this performance, the company has successfully implemented multiple transformations aimed at improving its innovation capabilities, developing world-class manufacturing operations, expanding into emerging markets, and reshaping its leadership model.

To support these initiatives, the company has adopted, and directly benefited from, several of the six imperatives discussed in this report. It has an explicit purpose – and the leadership team has taken steps to ensure that transformation programs are tightly linked to that purpose and that employees understand how their actions contribute to achieving that purpose. It also has a learning mindset and strong cross-functional collaboration, which are wired into the organization's processes and culture (and monitored through key performance indicators).

In addition, the company is taking steps to improve in several other important areas. Specifically, the leadership team has realized that setting the right pace and sequence of activities is critical to sustaining employees' energy across multiple transformations, and it has prioritized among the programs currently under way. It also recently assessed its capability gaps and launched a program to build the pivotal capabilities required to continue to grow while adapting to market dynamics. Recognizing the importance of change management, it has set up a transformation office led by a senior executive who holds responsibility for overseeing and integrating the various transformation initiatives and for building organization capabilities.

The company is also elevating, and reshaping, the role of HR into a strategic transformation partner – including appointing a senior executive to lead the function and redesigning the HR operating model to better support the company's transformation agenda. For its part, the leadership team has truly embraced its new transformational style and role – setting clear direction while being highly inclusive (rather than simply telling employees to "get with the program").

Through all of these actions, the company is taking deliberate steps to compete in a highly dynamic market, in which success comes not from any single transformation but from the ability to launch and implement multiple transformations over time.

---

2. **Ingrain the six imperatives.** In addition to applying the right style of leadership, leaders also have to chart the best path for ingraining the six imperatives into the company's organization and culture. While all six are important, management teams and organizations may not have the capacity to incorporate them all at once. Some will be more critical to a company's unique situation and to the types of transformation it is undergoing. For example, a company that already has a well-defined and articulated purpose need not spend time developing and communicating it but can move quickly to ensuring that the organization understands how the transformation links to it. Similarly, the pivotal capabilities required by a company that is launching a major operational improvement effort will be different from the capabilities needed by a company that is rolling out a digital initiative. A deliberate approach to prioritization and pace – as well as a thoughtful assessment of internal leadership and organizational bandwidth – will help leaders reach the best outcome.

The days of short-term, one-off transformations are ending. In this extremely dynamic business environment, we have reached the era of always-on transformation. The old approach – that is, top-down orders to employees, with enough oversight to hit short-term targets and declare victory – is no longer a viable option. Instead, companies need to launch near-continuous transformations across business units and functions.

Companies that integrate the six imperatives and adopt the HR and leadership roles outlined in this report should be well-positioned to gain sustainable improvements in performance from individual transformations and to ingrain the ability to transform repeatedly over time. Doing so is a significant challenge, but companies have little choice. They can cling to the old ways and become less relevant, or they can embrace a new approach that will enable them not just to survive but to thrive in the era of always-on transformation.

Martin Reeves, Julien Legrand, Jack Fuller, and Hen Lotan

Chapter 14
Free Up your Mind to Free Up your Strategy

Rates of change in business have never been so high: five-year EBIT margin volatility has jumped from 10% to 20% since the 1990s, and companies move through their business life cycles[1] twice as fast today as they did in the early 1990s.

Companies therefore need to anticipate change. There is strong evidence that preemptive self-disruption[2] is much more likely to be successful than involuntary disruption. But many forces mitigate against this, especially the conservatism and complacency that often follow success. Too often, when we need to be responsive to the environment, we end up following the same well-trodden paths in our processes and thinking.

We need the equivalent of a "fire starter" – something to kick-start our minds, to push us out of habitual process-driven ruts. We propose that well-designed games can serve this purpose, unlocking imagination and intelligence to take us to the starting line for developing great strategy.

Counterfactual Thinking

The idea of playing games in business may sound frivolous, but they can be a powerful tool to unlock a much-needed capacity: counterfactual thinking. Most of the time in business, we focus on the factual world – the dynamics that exist around us and the problems they raise. But it is sometimes vital to get away from what happens to be the case now (the factual) to consider imaginative possibilities (the counterfactual): the realm of what is not currently the case but could be.

Without counterfactual thinking, we become mentally and practically stuck. We focus only on exploiting the prevailing offering and business model instead of asking broader strategic questions: What other products and services could we

1 Martin Reeves, Sandy Moose, and Thijs Venema, "BCG Classics Revisited: The Growth Share Matrix," *BCG Publications*, June 4, 2014. https://www.bcg.com/publications/2014/growth-share-matrix-bcg-classics-revisited [accessed 9/5/2020].

2 Martin Reeves, Lars Fæste, Fabien Hassan, Harshal Parikh, and Kevin Whitaker, "Preemptive Transformation: Fix It Before It Breaks," *BCG Henderson Institute*, August 17, 2018. https://www.bcg.com/publications/2018/preemptive-transformation-fix-it-before-it-breaks [accessed 9/5/2020].

https://doi.org/10.1515/9783110697834-014

develop? How could our company transform itself? What scenarios might throw us off course or offer new opportunities?

We need to provoke counterfactual thinking in order to explore, learn, and change.

Former IBM CEO Lou Gerstner pointed out two major barriers to substantial change in large companies: the failure to create a sense of urgency and the failure to address entrenched interests. Games help overcome both these barriers. First, because we are tuned to deal with what is most immediate to us, there is usually no urgency to contemplate new possibilities. But by putting daily demands on hold, games create a context where thinking counterfactually becomes the priority. As well as the permission they give, the competition and excitement of games drive a sense of urgency.

Second, it often seems pointless to imagine possibilities for change if you don't believe that they could ever happen because of entrenched interests. Games address this barrier by creating an interaction in which entrenched interests are put aside, reducing the risk of suggesting new ideas. It is hard in a regular business meeting to ask hypothetically about transformation if the division head is sitting right there. In a game, you can playfully raise possibilities in a context that includes key stakeholders, but where everyone knows the thinking is exploratory.

Strategy Games

What are specific games we can play that will help us self-disrupt our thinking to get us to the starting line for constructing a creative strategy?

Strategy Palette

It is a common pitfall for companies to think of strategy too narrowly; the default is usually the classical "analyze, plan, and execute" approach. To explore a broader range of approaches, we created the *Strategy Palette Game*[3] (available on iOS and Android). In this game, you operate a lemonade stand in various competitive environments and must adapt your approach to strategy and execution accordingly. The game can be used as a starting point to discuss how different parts of your

---

3 "BCG Strategy Game teaser," *BHI, YouTube,* https://www.youtube.com/watch?v= XKyBEkHziuI [accessed 9/5/2020].

organization face different strategic environments, and understand why this in turn calls for a range of approaches to strategy and implementation.

This is true not only for companies but also for business units within a company. The game shows that a single standard process for strategy is no longer viable, hence inviting and legitimizing a broader set of approaches beyond planning.

Invert your Company

To play this game, first think through your current business model, identifying and articulating underlying assumptions. For example, a car manufacturer's business model might be based on the assumption that people want to buy cars, that cars will be manufactured in factories, that the main offering of the company is cars, and so on.

The next step is to invert these assumptions, either by reversing them or radically changing them in some way. Then imagine and make the best case for doing business on the basis of these inverted assumptions. For example, inverted assumptions could include: that people only rent cars (that the offering is a service, not a product) or that cars or parts are made by 3D printing in a decentralized fashion. The important thing is not to be right but to stretch your thinking to generate ideas that may be worthy of further consideration. An apparently ridiculous idea might indeed be unviable – or it may be merely unfamiliar and uncomfortable. It is not possible to discover valuable but uncomfortable ideas without first thinking counterfactually.

This game has two main intended outcomes: First, to make explicit the assumptions on which your business model is based. Second, to generate new ideas from the inverted company view to open up new possibilities and thinking paths.

Maverick Battle

For this game, first list all the companies, large and small, that are implicitly making a bet against your business model. Pick five that capture the range of alternative business model assumptions and imagine the implications of each becoming successful to the point of challenging your business. For example, a large real estate company might consider the disruptor Redfin. Though currently small, one could picture a future in which Redfin is a $5 billion firm, and its app-based model for bidding on houses is as popular as the prevailing model of using a real estate agent.

Then, imagining this future scenario, picture what your company would need to have done to compete successfully against the maverick. What strategic moves would your company have made, and what capabilities would it have developed or acquired? The point is not whether or not the maverick actually succeeds – most challengers, especially startups, will fail. Rather, the point is to test the disruptive potential of their ideas, stretch your thinking, and in so doing discover new threats and opportunities.

Doing this can lead to three useful outcomes. First, by imagining the means by which mavericks could succeed, you can better understand their ideas and selectively incorporate them into your own business model. Second, by considering potential future rivals, you can identify and prepare countermoves in advance. Third, you can broaden the set of ideas that form the starting point for strategy development and in so doing reduce the all-too-common danger that the result of your strategy process is merely a marginal variant of the status quo.

Destroy your Business

Select an area of your business and contemplate how to disrupt it. Playing the role of a disruptor, flesh out the details of a business model and how to go about realizing it.

The game surfaces your company's key vulnerabilities and identifies disruptors' potential moves and success factors. Once those have been identified, you can consider whether you want to integrate these elements into your own strategy. GE famously systematized the approach in the late 1990s, asking each of its units to have one "DestroyYourBusiness.com" team to come up with disruptive internet-based ideas. By adopting such an approach, companies can ensure an external-oriented and flexible mindset, which helps reduce the risk of being caught off-guard. This is critical, since research indicates that the single biggest predictor of success in major change is the timing of initiation.

Bad Customer

Imagine, or actually go and meet, people who do not use your products or services or who have major dissatisfactions with your business model. Try to put yourself inside their heads; make educated guesses about their desires, worries, and frustrations. Then brainstorm new ideas for business models that would satisfy these "bad customers."

It's satisfying to focus on current customers who like you. Almost by definition, your best, longest-standing customers appreciate you; but they may not be able to tell you very much about the disruptive ideas that could undermine your business model. A lot can be learned from the people who have quit your product or have no interest in it. For example, what would it take to convince an iPhone fan to purchase an Android phone? Or a Mac user to switch to a Windows computer? Disruption often starts from noncustomers, or marginal customers, and thus can provide a window into the future.

This game should lead to a better understanding of your company's weaknesses and self-imposed limits. By contemplating these, you not only alert yourself to possible threats but also discover untapped opportunities to expand your customer base or revitalize your business model.

Activist Attack

A common model when a private equity firm buys a company, for example 3G Capital's takeover of Heinz, is to fundamentally rethink the business and to strip out all unnecessary complexity and inefficiency. Rather than assuming the validity of the current way of doing things, as companies often do in their routine strategy process, activists start from a "blank sheet." Then they remove what is not part of the reimagined company.

Rather than waiting to be targeted or acquired by an aggressive PE firm or by activist investors, we can preemptively simulate such an attack. Imagine starting from zero in building your current company. What is strictly necessary to perform excellently and create loyal and satisfied customers? Once you have built up this picture, turn back to your current model and try to identify unnecessary complexity and cost. Some companies even hire advisors with long experience in PE or activist investing to help them keep the exercise honest.

Of course, your collective imagination around what you do and don't require for success isn't guaranteed to be right. But the game is a starting point for raising questions that the subsequent strategy process needs to address and generating options to free up resources to invest in growth.

Fix your Customer's Life

Amazon aims to "solve shopping" for its customers. That is, it has identified an area of its customers' lives and aims to solve any and all problems in this area, even if they have never been addressed or solved by any business before. In so doing, Amazon is framing needs that current customers may not even realize they have.

For this game, ask yourself what area of your customers' lives your company addresses. It is important to picture this holistically from the consumer's perspective, not from the narrower perspective of supplying today's products and services. For example, a bank is fundamentally concerned with solving money-related needs. An Amazon-like real-estate company would be aiming to "solve accommodation." This might include offering products and services we currently classify under interior design, construction, financing, hospitality, and travel – as well as services yet to be invented. These might include, for example, new psychological services to address questions such as when is the right time to move, why you want to move, and what you are truly looking for from a home as a function of your life stage and outlook.

Step back from current operations and products and think about the area of human life that your company touches. Think about the problems no one else has solved yet. This is the territory you could move into to build a winning strategy for the future.

Frictions

Imagine a business where customers experience no friction, a business in which there's perfect choice, perfect information, no search costs, perfect customer understanding of your offering, perfect availability, no mistakes, no quality issues or rework, and no delays. Then consider where your business departs from this ideal scenario. Quantify the cost involved and ask yourself: What are the sources of friction that are largest and easiest to reduce? Imagine a business model that would create this improved customer experience.

No business is frictionless, but disruptors, to have a viable and compelling proposition, will implicitly be addressing a source of friction that incumbents take for granted. It can be hard to identify such frictions, since the current business model may have decades of precedent. There may be no customers complaining about, nor competitors yet addressing, these frictions. Here are the sorts of questions you'd ask to uncover these frictions in an insurance company: Is it inevitable that there are many risks that are hard to insure, that insurance contracts are hard to understand, that it's hard for individuals to comprehend their total risk profile, that it's painful to adjust one's insurance portfolio, that intermediaries take substantial margins for providing navigation and advice, and that claims are resolved only after substantial delay? What questions would you need to ask about your business to reveal the frictions you take for granted?

The frictions game can help you envision sources of disruption preemptively, and surface ideas on how to better serve customers with more competitive and economically attractive business models.

Heroic Press Conference

Your company's new business venture has become immensely successful. Imagine the press conference explaining this success. What would it be like? What would you say about your company? Then consider what it took for the company to get there.

The heroic press conference game can align stakeholders on a vision of success and help elaborate the concrete steps required to reach it. There is a stage when a new innovation is known but may not yet be seriously contemplated as a future pillar of the business. Scaling an innovation requires not only increasing the resources allocated to it and removing the bottlenecks to expanding operational scale, but also cultivating belief and adoption by employees, customers, and investors. Working backward from the counterfactual of assumed success can help create the narrative that brings this about.

Preemptive Postmortem

Come up with a couple of plausible catastrophic events (such as natural disasters or competitive disruptions) and think about how your current or contemplated strategy would be impacted.

The effectiveness of a new strategy can be hard to assess. Confronting it with dramatic events is a great way to further push the thinking, making it more robust. In today's business world, the longevity of a strategy is as important as its immediate attractiveness.

The game lets participants identify risks to take into account when further developing the strategy, identify the conditions under which it could fail, and develop the actions required to mitigate these.

Combining Games

The games described above can be leveraged in various combinations depending on your company's situation and needs: you can choose to use one, several, or all of the games as part of your strategy process. You can use the games as a prelude to a formal strategy process or even as an alternative to a more traditional process.

For example, here are several combinations of games that address common business needs:

- *Rethink the Company's Strategic Direction:* Start with Strategy Palette, followed by Invert Your Company, Activist Attack, Heroic Press Conference, and Preemptive Postmortem.
- *Identify and React to Potential Disruptive Threats:* Start with Strategy Palette, followed by Maverick Battle, Frictions, Destroy Your Business, and Activist Attack.
- *Enhance Customer Focus:* Start with Strategy Palette, followed by Bad Customer, Frictions, and Fix Your Customer's Life.
- *Foster Alignment Around and Elaboration of a New Strategy:* Start with Strategy Palette, followed by Heroic Press Conference.

How to Run Strategy Games Effectively

Running games successfully requires the right environment, the right mindset, and the right participants.

Playfulness happens when people feel comfortable enough to think freely, allowing established ideas and interests to be challenged. The "playground" needs to be a judgment-free area, favoring suggestion and elaboration over argumentation. This can be helped by escaping the traditional meeting room, which can signal business as usual.

But changing the space is only effective when it is accompanied by a change in mindset. This comes from the top: managers should be careful to suspend judgment and encourage others to do the same. "The best way to have a good idea is to have a lot of ideas," says Nobel Prize winner Linus Pauling. Judgment can occur after the game, once the development of a strategy begins. Counterfactual thinking works by elaboration and thus requires patience and a constructive approach. The starting points are often vague or odd – before the picture gets filled in.

Success with games, finally, relies on selecting the right players. Participants should include those with the power to act on the ideas or influence those who can. It should ideally also involve a diversity of viewpoints: different positions within the company, business units, and cognitive styles. Yet the greater diversity in positions (such as the CEO and an associate in the same room), the more attention is required to mindset in order to ensure that people feel able to contribute.

Running games as a precursor to the strategy process can free up the precious resources of our minds, which determines how other resources are subsequently used. Games take us beyond habitual assumptions and processes, and set the ground for reading critical changes in the business environment and responding with creative new strategies.

Jim Hemerling, Julie Kilmann, and Dave Matthews

Chapter 15
The Head, Heart, and Hands
of Transformation

It is rare these days, as digital transformation sweeps the business landscape, to meet a business leader who hasn't either recently led or been part of a transformation. Once a one-off event in response to an urgent need – a dire competitive threat, sagging performance, an overdue process overhaul, or a post-merger integration – transformation is now the new normal. In fact, it has become so commonplace that we have dubbed this the era of "always-on" transformation.

Yet from experience we know that transformation continues to be very difficult, and the evidence shows that it often fails or falls short of expectations. Moreover, it can exact an enormous toll on leaders and employees, who are constantly being asked to step up, reach further, move faster, and adapt to change, with no end in sight. For leaders and employees alike, it's less a marathon and more a triathlon; no sooner does one leg finish than another is under way, giving participants no chance to catch their breath before giving their all once again. Still, many organizations overcome the odds; some even achieve lasting results. How do these companies succeed where others fail?

A Reimagined Approach to Transformation

While there is no one-size-fits-all method, our extensive client work, along with our study of more than 100 companies that have undergone transformations (three or more for 85% of them), points to an approach that combines three interconnected elements. It involves thinking expansively and creatively about the future that the organization aspires to and focusing on the right strategic priorities to get there. It addresses the unrelenting, ever-shifting, ever-growing demands on employees by elevating the importance of actions that will inspire and empower people at all levels of the organization; and at a time of rapid change and disruption, it calls for more than just applying the appropriate means and tools to execute; it calls for companies to innovate *while* they execute – and do both with agility.

In other words, transformation in the new digital era requires a holistic, human-centric approach, one we call the Head, Heart, and Hands of

https://doi.org/10.1515/9783110697834-015

Transformation. The heart has received the least consideration, but it is attention to all three elements that enables organizations to succeed today and thrive tomorrow.

Three Challenges in the Always-on Era

Transformation today takes place from a variety of starting positions. Some organizations need to move quickly to improve the bottom line. Others enjoy respectable performance but lack a clear path to enduring success. Many companies are simply in need of rejuvenation, ready to imagine a new destiny and perhaps even to increase their contribution to society.

Transforming not merely to survive but to thrive entails addressing three broad challenges, crystallized in these questions:

1. **How do we create our vision for the future and identify the priorities to get there?** Many companies face an even bigger challenge than overcoming short-term performance pressures: How to reconcile multiple strategic options to envision a different future amid shifting customer needs, evolving technologies, and increasing competition.

2. **How do we inspire and empower people?** The relentless pace of always-on transformation can demoralize even the most engaged employees. Sustaining it while offering employees meaningful opportunity and fulfillment – intrinsic rewards that millennials and "digital natives" seek – adds substantial complexity to the challenge.

3. **How do we execute amid constant change?** Changing the business once meant executing from a playbook of primarily short-term, discrete actions. But transforming to thrive in the future often requires disrupting existing business models and value chains to solve customer needs – and doing so at digital speed. Today, when changing the business means simultaneously executing and innovating with agility, a conventional approach to execution is no longer enough.

Taken together, these three challenges can seem overwhelming. But they need not be.

Consider Microsoft. In February 2014, when Satya Nadella took the helm, the company was by no means broken, yet there were strong headwinds: Windows' market share had declined, Microsoft had missed the mobile wave, and competitors – and customers – were moving aggressively to the cloud. The company's inhospitable culture was depicted in a now-famous meme showing managers in different corners of the organization chart shooting guns at one another.

Since then, Microsoft's performance hasn't just improved; it has flourished. Revenues (particularly cloud-based revenues) have soared, the company's stock price has more than tripled, market capitalization is approaching $1 trillion, and annualized TSR, at 26.5%, is twice that of the S&P 500. Perhaps most important, the company now boasts a visibly new culture of cooperation and a renewed commitment to innovation.

Microsoft's wholesale transformation has been the result not of a single move but of many changes orchestrated in parallel that have touched every part of the organization. Nadella honed a mobile-first, cloud-first vision, aligning leaders around it and shifting resources toward the relevant businesses to accelerate innovation. In other words, he addressed the *head* of transformation. He articulated a new purpose – "to empower every person and organization on the planet to achieve more" – and fostered a new culture and leadership model, thus tending to the *heart* of transformation. He also unleashed new ways of working that have not only enabled execution but also have spurred innovation and agility; that is, he equipped the *hands* of transformation.

Microsoft's transformation has reinvigorated a maturing company, positioning it to define and embrace its future with the strength and agility needed to thrive in a fast-changing, tumultuous business landscape.

The Power of Head, Heart, and Hands

What actions constitute this fresh take on transformation? And what sets it apart from more traditional approaches?

The Head: Envision the Future and Focus on the Big Rocks

In the digital era, constant change makes it harder to commit to a view of the future, but providing direction to the organization remains essential. That means companies and their leaders must draw on their strategic thinking, their imagination, their knowledge of customer needs and desires, and their pool of expertise, experience, and wisdom to forge an aspirational vision of a digitally enabled, growth-oriented future. They set priorities, focusing on the "big rocks" that will deliver results and create enduring value.[1] They secure the alignment and commitment of the leadership team. And they establish and communicate a compelling case for change, internally and externally. In the past, these actions might have been one-and-done moves, distinct from the daily rhythms of business; but today, because the environment is constantly shifting and these strategic actions generally affect the whole enterprise, they must be revisited and updated on an ongoing basis (ideally, annually) and be integrated into the operating model of the organization.

The Heart: Inspire and Empower your People

When transformations were viewed as one-off, short-term programs, inspiring and empowering people wasn't seen as being essential to them; in fact, people were often treated as a means to an end or, worse, as collateral damage. But successful transformation today depends on people who are engaged and motivated to go above and beyond their day-to-day operations. Organizations can create this condition through a set of heart "practices." What does this mean? Leaders invest time and energy in articulating, activating, and embedding the organization's purpose. Companies create an empowering culture, shaped by leaders, that allows people to do their best work. They also demonstrate care for those whose lives are disrupted by the change – not only departing employees but those who remain to carry out the new vision. Finally, senior managers exercise a more holistic form of leadership: they clarify and navigate, they include and empower, and they delegate and enable their people and teams.

The Hands: Execute and Innovate with Agility

Executing a prescribed set of actions used to be enough to generate short-term bottom-line improvements. In this new era, when the future is unclear and the present is constantly changing, organizations need to innovate as they execute, and do both with agility. Consider this: Rather than delegate responsibility for execution to a transformation program owner (who occasionally updates leaders), companies give joint ownership of the ongoing transformation agenda to

---

1 "Big rocks" is a reference to Stephen Covey's famous demonstration of setting priorities: filling a large mason jar with rocks (the most important things), then gravel, then sand, and finally water (items of lesser importance that can be fit in).

senior leaders. They ensure disciplined execution by equipping teams with the resources they need to make sound, prompt decisions. Companies also apply innovative methods and digital tools, and institute agile ways of working to accelerate output, remove impediments, and enable end-to-end focus on the customer. Whereas building organizational capabilities was often an afterthought, today companies build capabilities while carrying out the transformation.

The head, heart, and hands approach to transformation is most powerful when each element is fully deployed. For this reason, the three elements should not be viewed as sequential actions but as three vital sets of activities that should happen in parallel – a holistic system.

Evidence of the impact of this approach is striking. In our study, which included in-depth interviews of leaders involved in these efforts, we asked whether the companies had addressed actions consistent with the three elements. We then correlated the response with their subsequent performance. Ninety-six percent of the companies that fully engaged the three elements achieved sustained performance improvement, a rate nearly three times that of companies that did not engage the elements (Figure 15.1).

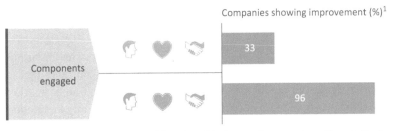

1. Improvement is defined as "breakthrough" or " Strong" Performance improvement as self-reported ins Survey
Source: BCG analysis

Figure 15.1: The Head, Heart, and Hands Together Make a Difference.

When we asked survey respondents about the relative attention given to each of the three elements during transformation, the head consistently got the highest rating, followed by the hands. The heart came last (Figure 15.2).

It's thus only fitting that the heart – as the metaphorical center and source of inspiration and power – is at the center of this holistic approach.

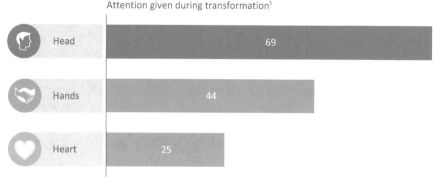

1. These numbers represent a measure akin to the Net Promoter Score, expressed as the balance of agrees (positive) vs. disagrees (negative) to questions about the presence of features of head, hands, and heart. It is computed as follows: Sum of agree and strongly agree minus the sum of disagree, strongly disagree, and neither agree nor disagree, normalized by all non-N/A responses. Its scale is +100% to -100%
Source: BCG analysis

Figure 15.2: The Hands and Heart Are Neglected in Transformations.

The Heart of Transformation: Inspire and Empower Your People

People – individuals and teams – are the lifeblood of successful transformation. Transformation requires their effort, engagement, alignment, and willingness to go the extra mile. But in practice, the importance of people in transformation is often neglected – people often end up being treated as expedient or even dispensable. In the always-on era, the consequences of this neglect can be great, as people grow exhausted from keeping up with the latest technologies and adapting to relentless change.

Successful transformation takes heart. The heart serves as an apt metaphor, capturing the essence of the vital, life-giving source of power that people need to effect change.

So how can organizations develop a strong, healthy heart to inspire and empower people? In the context of transformation, we see four imperatives. Each of them, like the chambers of the heart, works in concert to perform the complete job: empowering and enabling people to give life to the transformation.

Healthy Heart, Strong Performance

The heart's impact on transformation results is measurable – and compelling. In our survey, we derived "heart scores" for companies based on their responses to a battery of questions about the characteristics and impact of their transformations. Among the companies that experienced strong sustained performance, the proportion with high heart scores was more than double the proportion of those with low heart scores. Moreover, a substantial proportion of low scorers performed more poorly at the end of the transformation than at its start (Figure 15.3).

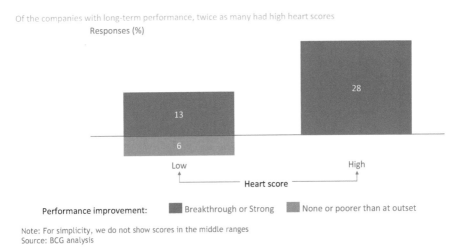

Of the companies with long-term performance, twice as many had high heart scores

Responses (%)

Performance improvement: ■ Breakthrough or Strong   ■ None or poorer than at outset

Note: For simplicity, we do not show scores in the middle ranges
Source: BCG analysis

Figure 15.3: The Heart Is Critical for Achieving and Sustaining Performance.

Activate and Embed Purpose

Increasingly, employees seek much more than a paycheck or tangible rewards; they want meaning, connection, and joy. They want to contribute, develop, and achieve. Organizations with purpose tap into these needs, producing a virtuous circle of benefits.

Purpose is an organization's "why" – its existential reason for being. In the always-on era, it is more important than ever; it fuels transformation by fostering an emotional connection that inspires greater commitment and the willingness to go the extra mile. Purpose illuminates a direction[2] as it links various transformation efforts in a way that is logical and accessible to everyone. But it can do so only when the organization translates it effectively into action.

Create an Empowering Culture

Culture is the essence of the organization. It comprises a clear articulation of the values and behaviors that define how things get done in an organization. Activated by leaders, culture is reinforced by the organizational environment, or context, through such levers as customer service rituals, performance management systems, and informal interactions. A healthy culture serves as a tacit code of conduct that steers individuals to make choices that advance the organization's goals and strategy. In the digital era, when self-direction and team autonomy are emphasized, a strong culture[3] is particularly important.

Demonstrate Care

Layoffs, redeployments, and reskilling are inevitable today. Even healthy companies will likely have to restructure their workforce to add talent – in particular, people with digital skills and experience that align more closely with the business's future needs. Such workforce turbulence can be traumatic not only for those who are laid off but also for those who remain. If left unattended, it can undermine morale and progress. At the very least, transformation can dampen engagement and disrupt employee cohesion, and it almost always puts extra demands on people.

For all these reasons, leaders must demonstrate care, compassion, and empathy – and not just through their words. For example, it is critical that leaders continue to solicit the input of employees who remain (say, through pulse checks or broader two-way communications) and actively, visibly address their

---

2 Cathy Carlisi, Jim Hemerling, Julie Kilmann, Dolly Meese, and Doug Shipman, "Purpose with the Power to Transform Your Organization," *BCG Publications*, May 15, 2017. https://www.bcg.com/publications/2017/transformation-behavior-culture-purpose-power-transform-organization [accessed 9/5/2020].

3 Jim Hemerling, Julie Kilmann, Martin Danoesastro, Liza Stutts, and Cailin Ahern, "It's Not a Digital Transformation Without a Digital Culture," *BCG Publications*, April 13, 2018. https://www.bcg.com/publications/2018/not-digital-transformation-without-digital-culture [accessed 9/5/2020].

concerns. To help employees who are leaving, companies can offer a battery of program options beyond the standard outplacement services, such as coaches to help individuals create a personal roadmap, job-market information sessions, resources for financial advice, and even guidance on entrepreneurship.

Lead with the Head, Heart, and Hands

Nothing is more important to the success of transformation than leaders. While they play many roles, leaders embody the heart of transformation.

- *Leaders Clarify and Navigate the Way Forward:* Beyond envisioning the future and revisiting strategic priorities regularly, leaders provide constant guidance to their reports and unit heads and ensure that priorities remain linked to purpose. They are action-oriented; they set clear accountabilities; and they work tirelessly to communicate a compelling case for change internally and externally.
- *Leaders Are Inspiring, Empowering, and Inclusive:* Leaders instill confidence and courage, and motivate and inspire people to perform. They strengthen and encourage teams and support cross-organization collaboration. They demonstrate care and empathy, actively and candidly communicate with their people, and exercise inclusiveness.
- *Leaders Delegate and Enable Agile Teams:* Leaders delegate responsibilities to autonomous agile teams, remove obstacles, and ensure all the necessary cross-functional resources are in place. They also support capabilities building, both human and digital.

Embracing the Head, Heart, and Hands of Transformation

In the digital era, transformation has become the default state for most organizations. But always-on transformation needn't be debilitating, exhausting, or demoralizing. We owe it to ourselves, our organizations, and society itself to boldly revolutionize the approach we take to transformation.

Leaders need to move beyond short-term fixes to envision a compelling future, and focus on the big rocks required to get there. They need to stop treating people as a means to an end or, worse, as collateral damage, and instead inspire and empower them. They need to change how work gets done, moving from the expedient and prescribed set of actions to an approach that enables execution and innovation to occur simultaneously, with agility.

The head, heart, and hands of transformation is not a panacea, but it is a holistic and human-centric approach that is proven to enable organizations that truly embrace it to succeed today and thrive tomorrow.

Martin Reeves and Kevin Whitaker
Chapter 16
Digital Transformations: Disruptions, Delusions, and Defenses

Disruptions

Incumbent businesses are right to be paranoid about the expanding impact of technological disruption. Of the top ten global companies by market capitalization a decade ago, only two have maintained their positions;[1] many of the rest were replaced by digital natives, and we expect the list ten years from now to be at least as different from today's: we know that only one-third of companies faced with industry disruption thrive,[2] while the remaining two-thirds languish or fail. It is not surprising, then, that incumbents in many sectors are engaged in extensive digital transformation efforts in an attempt to inoculate themselves against the threat of disruption.

Our research has shown that three-quarters of large-scale change efforts fail to meet their objectives.[3] Digital transformations are among the riskiest for established businesses because of the depth and breadth of change involved, the capability disadvantage of many incumbents, the pace at which digital disruption can unfold, and the fact that customers' expectations are typically set by a digital native like Amazon or Netflix rather than a direct competitor. Given the high stakes, it's important to consider how such efforts are structured and executed in order to avoid a number of common pitfalls.

---

1 BCG Henderson Institute, "Winners are Changing Rapidly – Chart of the Week #15 / 2019," April 12, 2019. https://bcghendersoninstitute.com/winners-are-changing-rapidly-chart-of-the-week-15-2019-33e9ce28d331 [accessed 9/5/2020].
2 Eric Wick, Jody Foldesy, and Sam Farley, "Creating Value from Disruption (While Others Disappear)," *BCG Publication*, 2017. https://www.bcg.com/publications/2017/value-creation-strategy-transformation-creating-value-disruption-others-disappear [accessed 9/5/2020].
3 Martin Reeves, Lars Fæste, Kevin Whitaker, and Fabien Hassan, "The Truth About Corporate Transformation: Empirical analysis reveals that conventional wisdom about big, risky change initiatives is often wrong." *MIT Sloan Management Review*, January 31, 2018. https://sloanreview.mit.edu/article/the-truth-about-corporate-transformation/ [accessed 9/5/2020].

https://doi.org/10.1515/9783110697834-016

Delusions

Several traps can derail the effectiveness of a digital transformation:

- *Wait-and-See Trap*: The evidence from hundreds of transformation efforts shows that the single biggest factor influencing success is how soon they are initiated.[4] In theory, effort could be wasted by starting too early and better-informed by starting later. In practice, however, companies tend to wait too long and would be better served by preemptively disrupting themselves. This is especially true when it comes to adopting digital business models, which can scale extremely rapidly.

- *Favorite-Modality Trap*: The managerial literature has focused sequentially on big data, predictive analytics, and artificial intelligence. But overemphasizing any single modality obscures more fundamental competitive and customer considerations. It also undermines the advantage of creating an integrated learning model, which requires ecosystems, sensors, data, analytics, and decision making all to be adopted in a coherent and connected manner.

- *Digitizing-Yesterday's-Model Trap*: Digital technology can create more-efficient processes by improving accuracy and reducing cost. Technological disruption rarely proceeds by competing on process efficiency, however. New customer value is usually created through new offerings and business models, which make existing processes obsolete rather than improve them.

- *Technology Centricity Trap*: Technology is the predominant driver of change in today's business world. But new technologies create little value if they don't address new or existing customer needs, with a superior business model. Digital transformation cannot therefore be driven primarily by the technology function. Furthermore, the current wave of AI is reshaping the relationship between humans and machines.[5] Hierarchy cannot be allowed to become the bottleneck in digitized business models, vested interests cannot be allowed to prevent appropriate technological substitution, human capabilities must be focused on higher-level cognitive tasks, and better human–machine interfaces are needed – challenges that span all aspects of management and organization.

---

4 Martin Reeves, Lars Fæste, Fabien Hassan, Harshal Parikh, and Kevin Whitaker, "Preemptive Transformation: Fix It Before It Breaks," *BCG Henderson Institute*, August 17, 2018. https://www.bcg.com/publications/2018/preemptive-transformation-fix-it-before-it-breaks [accessed 9/5/2020].
5 Allison Bailey, Martin Reeves, Kevin Whitaker, and Rich Hutchinson, "The Company of the Future: Winning the '20s," *BCG Henderson Institute*, April 5, 2019. https://www.bcg.com/publications/2019/company-of-the-future [accessed 9/5/2020].

- *Beating-the-Competition Trap*: As a famous joke goes, if you and another hiker are being chased by a bear, you don't need to outrun the bear to survive – you just need to outrun the other hiker. Similarly, when assessing their digital transformation efforts, leaders may naturally use their traditional competitors as benchmarks. But as the concept of an industry becomes increasingly tenuous, this mindset is no longer sufficient. Many technological disruptors are invaders from other industries. Furthermore, customers' expectations of digital interfaces and offerings will more likely be set by their interactions with Amazon or Alibaba than by what the other companies in your industry are doing. The competitive standard should therefore be set by the digital leaders, not industry peers.
- *Customer Satisfaction Trap*: Existing customers will, almost by definition, be satisfied with your current offering – so traditional customer research is likely to give the impression that there is little risk of disruption. However, your digital competitors are probably aiming to satisfy latent needs that today's customers may not be aware of. High customer satisfaction scores therefore should not be grounds for complacency.
- *One-and-Done Trap*: Technology continues to evolve, and many industries have already seen several cycles in which the disruptors have themselves been disrupted. Our recent research on digital ecosystems shows that this is the norm rather than the exception. Transformation thus should not be a one-shot effort – organizations must instead build capabilities for *continual* change.

Defenses

How, then, can incumbents effectively defend their positions and increase their odds of success in digital transformation? We suggest several imperatives for effective digital transformation:

- *Eliminate Customer Frictions*: Frictions include any unnecessary costs, delays, mistakes, misunderstandings, or dissatisfactions that a customer may experience. Often they seem to be invisible, because they are longstanding and accepted, and there may be no obvious alternative. But such frictions are likely to be the place where a disruptor will attack. So an exercise that compares the status quo with a hypothetical frictionless version of your industry, and identifies the most valuable and tractable sources of friction, can be critical in guiding digital transformation.

- *Preemptively Self-Disrupt:* Given the long odds of surviving disruption, companies should not wait for an external challenge to act. Instead, they should preemptively "self-disrupt" to avoid being pushed into a defensive and reactionary stance, from where it might be impossible to catch up.
- *Learn from "Mavericks":* Clues for how to self-disrupt can be found by examining the value propositions and business models of mavericks on the edge of your industry or in neighboring industries and asking, what if they were successful? By getting inside their worldview, you can surface ideas about how your current business model might need to be evolved or whether it should be replaced. Taking the perspective of mavericks forces outside-in competitive thinking in a way that internal speculation cannot.
- *Autonomize:* To leverage the power of AI and compete on learning[6] – the ability to identify new insights and act accordingly – you need to move beyond mere automation of existing processes. Instead, you should create hands-off learning by connecting proprietary data, pattern-detecting AI, and automated decision making. This also means getting the hierarchy out of the way by creating a new organizational model based on autonomous learning loops.
- *Beat the Best:* Understand who is setting the standards for digital customer experience beyond your industry, and exceed those standards in building your self-disruptive model. Survivors of industry disruption are usually differentiated not by the uniqueness of their approaches, but by their rigor and scale.
- *Destroy Your Business:* Organizations naturally resist change. This resistance is usually strongest when it comes to defending the power structures and resource pools associated with legacy business models. Leaders thus need to go well beyond asking the neutral question, "How could we do better?" Instead, they can have key stakeholders simulate the destruction of their business model at the hands of potential disruptors, an exercise that is more likely to raise the key underlying issues and possibilities.
- *Leverage Your Strengths:* The first wave of digital disruption attacked relatively easy B2C targets with predominantly digital models. The next wave, which will include B2B players, will likely follow a very different logic,[7] in which relationships, organizational navigation, specialized knowledge,

---

6 Martin Reeves and Kevin Whitaker, "Competing on the Rate of Learning," *BCG Henderson Institute*, August 24, 2018. https://www.bcg.com/en-us/publications/2018/competing-rate-learning [accessed 9/5/2020].

7 Martin Reeves and Claudio Chittaro, "Getting Physical: The Rise of Hybrid Ecosystems," *BCG Henderson Institute*, September 15, 2017. https://www.bcg.com/publications/2017/business-model-innovation-technology-digital-getting-physical-rise-hybrid-ecosystems [accessed 9/5/2020].

and capital will be required in order to sell and service complex and expensive physical assets. Consequently, the next battle between incumbents and digital natives may be in some ways more evenly matched. Nevertheless, incumbents have no automatic right to be the orchestrator in an ecosystem, and some digital competitors will master the art of relationship management and selling specialized, capital-intensive assets and services. Incumbents must think about how they can leverage their historical advantages while self-disrupting their business models and building the capabilities to do so.

– *Build Perpetual Transformation Capabilities:* Digital transformation in many cases will not be the one-shot affair it is often assumed to be. Ecosystems coevolve, technology progresses, and competitive standards continually rise. Ongoing transformation skills are therefore necessary. Moreover, change will increasingly be based on data and analysis rather than rules of thumb and uniform recipes – so-called "evidence based transformation."[8] Digital transformers must therefore be masters of change management, too.

Responses to the threat and opportunity of digital disruption should not confuse means and ends. Technology may be the threat and the medium of change, but in the long run, only applications and organizational models that focus on competitive superiority will win.

---

8 By Lars Faeste, Martin Reeves, and Kevin Whitaker, "Winning the '20s: The Science of Change," BCG Henderson Institute, April 9, 2019. https://bcghendersoninstitute.com/winning-the-20s-the-science-of-change-95db378c5d91 [accessed 9/5/2020].

Gideon Walter, Mike Shanahan, Martin Reeves,
and Kaelin Goulet

Chapter 17
Why Transformations Need a Second Chapter

It's a well-known mantra in business: "You can't cut your way to greatness." Nonetheless, painful cost cutting and other defensive measures are a familiar strategy for staying afloat. They are quick and obvious and deliver tangible results, but they are not in themselves a recipe for success. What does a CEO driving a turnaround do after these "easy" measures have been exhausted? In an era in which markets are more turbulent and leadership is less durable, companies must continually renew their competitive advantage.[1]

It is not surprising that an increasing number of companies find themselves out of step with market realities and in need of transformation. As Xerox CEO Ursula Burns said in May 2012, "If you don't transform your company, you're stuck."[2] But transformation in its true sense – the restoration of vitality, growth, and competitiveness – is easier said than done. In fact, 75% of transformations ultimately fail (Figure 17.1). In practice, the visionary titles given to transformation programs – names like "Inspire" or "Phoenix" – are often mere euphemisms for cost reduction.

We looked closely at the long-term performance of transformation programs by using the method of paired historical comparisons, an approach that eliminates interesting but irrelevant details and zeroes in on the key factors that separate success from failure. We studied a dozen pairs of companies, each in the same industry and facing similar challenges at similar times. Our study revealed two common trajectories: short-term recovery with long-term slow decline and, less commonly, short-term recovery with long-term restoration of growth and performance (Figure 17.2). So what's the formula for the second path?

---

1 See "Adaptability: The New Competitive Advantage," BCG article, August 2011. https://www.bcg.com/publications/2011/business-unit-strategy-growth-adaptability-the-new-competitive-advantage [accessed 9/5/2020].
2 "If You Don't Transform, You're Stuck," narrated by Renee Montagne, Morning Edition, *NPR*, May 23, 2012.

https://doi.org/10.1515/9783110697834-017

Long-term relative TSR growth

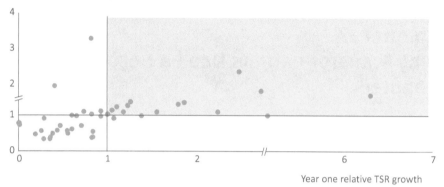

Year one relative TSR growth

Note: Based on a representative analysis 48 companies publicly undergoing corporate-transformation efforts. Total shareholder return(TSR) is adjusted by S&P 500 growth;1=same growth rate as the index. Long-term growth refers to a period of five years or a period that is ongoing (that is, transformations begun since July 2008) Source: BCG analysis

Figure 17.1: Seventy-five Percent of Transformations Ultimately Fail.

Chapter One: The Turnaround

In theory, companies could preemptively or continuously transform themselves, but that is not often what happens. All the examples we studied had a first phase of cost cutting and streamlining – triggered by a decline in competitive or financial performance – which we call chapter one of transformation. In chapter one, the fundamental goal is to do the same with less.

Chapter one does seem to be an essential component of transformation; we didn't find a single successful example that didn't go through this phase. Streamlining reduces inefficiencies, buys time by addressing short-term financial woes, and frees up resources to fund the journey toward future growth. A typical chapter one lasts up to about 18 months and is usually successful in restoring total shareholder returns to sector parity levels. The main mistake that some companies make during chapter one is not cutting boldly enough at the outset, which can trigger painful, repeated rounds of cost cutting and undermine morale, momentum, and leadership credibility.

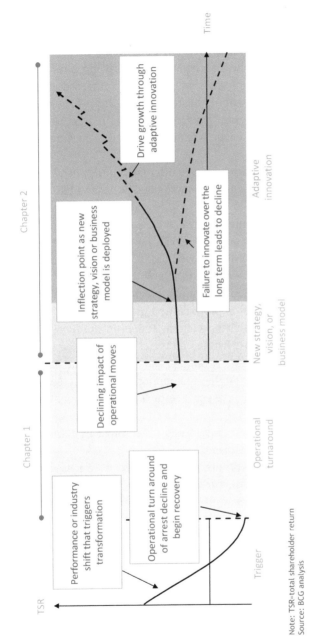

Figure 17.2: Two Common Transformation Trajectories.

Chapter Two: Creating Lasting Change

For successful transformers, though, the story doesn't end there. Of the companies we studied, those that thrived all had a distinct second phase of transformation: chapter two. Whereas chapter one primarily addressed costs, chapter two focused mainly on growth and innovation. In chapter two, successful companies went beyond necessary but insufficient operational improvements and deployed a new strategy, vision, or business model that they refined over a multiyear period.

Transformations don't follow a cookie-cutter model; they need to reflect the challenges unique to each situation. Nonetheless, we identified eight factors that drive long-term success:

1. **Turning the page.** Companies make a conscious decision to go beyond the efficiency moves of chapter one and refocus on growth and innovation.
2. **Creating a new vision**. Companies articulate a clear shift in strategic direction, coupled with room for experimentation.
3. **Foundational innovation**. They innovate across multiple dimensions of the business model, not just in products and processes.
4. **Commitment.** There is persistence from leaders in the face of inevitable setbacks and internal opposition to unproven shifts in strategy.
5. **Imposed distance.** There is a willingness to shift from the historical core business model and its underlying assumptions, often by creating a deliberate degree of separation between the new business model and legacy operations.
6. **Adaptive approach.** Transformation unfolds through trial and error, with ongoing refinement of a flexible plan.
7. **Shots on goal.** Companies do not pin growth hopes on a single move but rather on deploying a portfolio of moves to drive growth.
8. **Patience.** There is adherence to the vision over a multi-year period.

But what about those that try to transform but fail? Many companies run into several of the following traps, which are surprisingly obvious yet seemingly difficult to avoid:

- *Early-Wins Trap:* Companies declare premature victory after chapter one and fail to declare or develop a second chapter.
- *Efficiency Trap:* They continue with multiple rounds of cost cutting and efficiency improvement measures.
- *Legacy Trap:* They fail to shed core assumptions and practices even when they are self-limiting or no longer relevant.

- *Proportionality Trap:* They make promising moves – such as a series of new business pilots – that are not proportionate to the scale of the challenge. "Dabbling" was a surprisingly common differentiator between the successful and unsuccessful companies we studied.
- *False Certainty Trap:* They believe that the course of action can be rigorously planned in advance, and they overemphasize disciplined implementation of a fixed plan instead of continually iterating in response to new knowledge.
- *Persistency Trap:* Companies underestimate the time needed to see results (often up to a decade), and, consequently, they let up too soon.
- *Proximity Trap:* They undermine the new business by keeping it too close to the core business, even when that closeness triggers competition for resources or conflicting assumptions.

Chapter Two in Practice

A close read of select case studies illustrates how chapter two can drive success or failure. The Australian airline Qantas's creation of Jetstar demonstrates a successful transformation through foundational innovation. Kodak illustrates the perils of a missed opportunity for a strategic turnaround. And IBM exemplifies how transformation must be managed over an inconveniently long time horizon.

A New Route for Qantas

In 2000, two low-cost carriers disrupted the Australian domestic-aviation market – a historic duopoly controlled by Ansett and Qantas. Twelve months later, Ansett collapsed and Qantas, a traditional airline with a high cost structure, was losing market share. From 2003 to 2010, however, Qantas's TSR outperformed both the market and the sector. How?

Qantas first commenced a transformation program to streamline operations, cutting $1 billion in costs over two years. Qantas then layered on chapter two – a fundamentally different business model – with its launch of Jetstar, a wholly owned, no-frills, low-cost carrier. Today, Jetstar is a core driver of Qantas Group's profit.

Chapter two worked because Qantas stayed focused on a key success factor for low-cost carriers: high-asset utilization – that is, maximizing the hours a plane operates, which enables the airline to charge lower fares. Qantas kept Jetstar's network and value proposition intentionally separate from its full-service offering, and it branded Jetstar distinctly for the leisure traveler. With its own fleet and profit-and-loss statement – and interactions with Qantas only at the board level – Jetstar flourished unencumbered by the legacy organization and cost structure. Further, a leadership team drawing heavily on external talent brought fresh thinking, flexibility, and a cultural shift to enable the new model.

International competitors undertook similar cost-reduction and low-cost-carrier launch efforts. But by the middle of the first decade of the twenty-first century, many such ventures were grounded. Falling into several of the common transformation traps, these new ventures were often too encumbered by core business cost structures or thinking to be effective and viable.

Kodak: A Missed Photo OP

Few brands were as synonymous with their industry as Kodak. So it was a sad end of an era when the company filed for bankruptcy in 2012. Kodak made a genuine effort to transform; it just didn't do so thoroughly or nimbly enough. In early September 2013, the company emerged from bankruptcy but as a much smaller operation with an unclear path forward.

Kodak's chapter one was characterized by multiple, insufficient rounds of cuts and layoffs, steps that degraded morale and failed to attract talent to fuel innovation. At the same time, even though Kodak had clearly identified a compelling opportunity – a shift to affordable digital cameras – it did not allocate sufficient resources to develop and expand this new strategy. Falling into the persistency trap, Kodak stifled new projects that did not meet the benchmark economics of its existing legacy film business. The culture of the legacy business prevailed with digital efforts integrated within the company, leaving Kodak ill-equipped to shift to a new business model.

IBM: Updating the Operating System

IBM's transformation is compelling for the persistency and success of its chapter two efforts. Since Big Blue embarked on a full transformation more than two decades ago, the company has undergone a chapter one operational turnaround; adopted a new strategy, business model, and vision; and – most critically – supported adaptive innovation despite changes in leadership and the environment. Three CEOs and two market crashes later, IBM's revenue has nearly doubled.

IBM engineered continuous transformation into its organizational DNA. Management displayed a clear vision for the future, pragmatically shifting its business toward high-margin services and software while shedding the lower-margin, lower-growth hardware business. The company ensured many shots on goal by empowering teams to innovate and build new businesses through a structured process, including incubating emerging business opportunities under separate management. And leadership has taken a long view and communicated it actively, going so far as to share four-year financial roadmaps with investors and analysts.

Transformation Paradox

In our study of transformation efforts, we see a remarkable paradox. The pitfalls of transformation are unsurprising, the payoff from doing things right is significant, the goals of transformation are clear – and yet organizations repeatedly fail to follow the right path to success.

There are multiple plausible reasons for this. For one thing, short-term cost cutting is easy and provides immediate rewards – and it's tempting to believe that more of the same will yield more of the same. In addition, risk-taking may seem unpalatable at the very moment you are grasping for stability. Leaders can be uncomfortable making the abrupt shift from cost cutting to the discipline of a growth strategy. The key to new growth will almost by definition seem counterintuitive – especially to the architects of the current business model. Indeed, the two chapters require very different leadership styles and capabilities, one more top-down and operational and the other more creative and empowering.

Leaders on the cusp of a transformation, therefore, need to embrace some inconvenient truths. Transformation demands attention to both the short term and the long term, to efficiency as well as innovation and growth, to discipline and flexible adaptation, and to clarity of direction and empowerment. Successful transformation requires an ambidexterity of leadership, one that resolves these apparent contradictions and navigates the company successfully through both chapters of transformation.[3]

---

3 See "Ambidexterity: The Art of Thriving in Complex Environments," *BCG Perspective*, February 2013. https://www.bcg.com/publications/2011/business-unit-strategy-growth-adaptability-the-new-competitive-advantage [accessed 9/5/2020].

List of Figures

https://doi.org/10.1515/9783110697834-018

Index

https://doi.org/10.1515/9783110697834-019